Financial Accounting and Reporting Requirements in Life Insurance Companies

LOMA (Life Office Management Association, Inc.) is an international association founded in 1924. LOMA is committed to a business partnership with its worldwide members in the insurance and financial services industry to improve their management and operations through quality employee development, research, information sharing, and related products and services. Among LOMA's activities is the sponsorship of the FLMI Education Program—an educational program intended primarily for home office and branch office employees.

The *FLMI Education Program* consists of two levels—Level I, *Fundamentals of Life and Health Insurance*, and Level II, *Functional Aspects of Life and Health Insurance*. Level I is designed to help students achieve a working knowledge of the life and health insurance business. Level II is designed to provide a more detailed understanding of life and health insurance and related business and management subjects. Students who complete Level I receive a certificate. Students who complete both levels earn the designation Fellow, Life Management Institute (FLMI) and receive a diploma.

Statement of Purpose: LOMA Educational Programs Testing and Designations

Examinations described in the *LOMA Education and Training Catalog* are designed solely to measure whether students have successfully completed the relevant assigned curriculum, and the attainment of the FLMI and other LOMA designations indicates only that all examinations in the given curriculum have been successfully completed. In no way shall a student's completion of a given LOMA course or attainment of the FLMI or other LOMA designation be construed to mean that LOMA in any way certifies that student's competence, training, or ability to perform any given task. LOMA's examinations are to be used solely for general educational purposes, and no other use of the examinations or programs is authorized or intended by LOMA. Furthermore, it is in no way the intention of the LOMA Curriculum and Examinations staff to describe the standard of appropriate conduct in any field of the insurance and financial services industry, and LOMA expressly repudiates any attempt to so use the curriculum and examinations. Any such assessment of student competence or industry standards of conduct should instead be based on independent professional inquiry and the advice of competent professional counsel.

Financial Accounting and Reporting Requirements in Life Insurance Companies

Elizabeth A. Mulligan, FLMI, ACS, ALHC, AIAA, PAHM

Information That Works

FLMI Education Program
Life Management Institute LOMA
Atlanta, Georgia
www.loma.org

Information in this text may have been changed or updated since its publication date. For current updates, visit www.loma.org.

FLMI 361 Text — **Financial Accounting and Reporting Requirements in Life Insurance Companies**

Author:	Elizabeth A. Mulligan, FLMI, ACS, ALHC, AIAA, PAHM
Manuscript Editor:	Susan Conant, FLMI, HIA, CEBS, PAHM
Exam Editor:	Cynthia Mathis Henry, FLMI, ALHC, ACS, PAHM
Project Manager:	Jena L. Kennedy FLMI, ALHC, ACS, CLU, PAHM
Production Manager:	Michelle Stone Weathers, ACS
Copyeditor and Indexer:	Robert D. Land, FLMI, ACS
Production Coordinator:	Allison Ayers
Print Coordinator:	Amy Souwan
Print Buyer:	Audrey M. Hiers
Permissions Coordinator:	Iris F. Hartley, FLMI, ALHC
Administrative Support:	Mamunah Carter Aurelia K. Hemphill Marion Markus
Cover Design:	Allison Ayers Michelle Stone Weathers, ACS
Cover Image:	© W. Whitehurst, CSM.

Library of Congress Cataloging-in-Publication Data

Mulligan, Elizabeth A.
   Financial accounting and reporting requirements in life insurance companies / Elizabeth A. Mulligan.
     p. cm.
   ISBN 1-57974-149-5
     1. Insurance, Life-Accounting. 2. Insurance, Life--United States--Accounting. 3. Insurance, Life--Canada--Accounting. I. Title.

   HG8848 .M854 2002
   657'.836--dc21   2001038469

ISBN 1-57974-149-5

Printed in the United States of America

Contents

Preface

Many individuals have provided valuable expertise that made this book possible. The membership of LOMA's Education Council, comprised of industry volunteers acting on behalf of the LOMA membership, identifies the membership's most urgent needs in the area of education and directs the LOMA staff to meet those needs. The combined efforts of many highly qualified experts supported the development of *Financial Accounting and Reporting Requirements in Life Insurance Companies*. On behalf of LOMA and its membership, we would like to express appreciation to those individuals who generously gave their time and energy and shared their considerable expertise for the development of this textbook.

Textbook Development Panel

Because, with permission from the publisher, *Financial Accounting and Reporting Requirements in Life Insurance Companies* draws heavily upon research originally conducted for a LOMA textbook that preceded it, we first thank the industry experts who served on the textbook development panel for and made enormous contributions to *Accounting and Financial Reporting in Life and Health Insurance Companies*, Elizabeth A. Mulligan and Gene Stone (Atlanta: LOMA, 1997):

- Thomas Allen, CPA, FLMI
- Alan E. Close, CPA, FLMI
- Larry J. Esposito, CPA, FLMI
- Susan I. Flynn, CGA, FLMI, ACS, AIAA
- Jerry Hogya, FLMI
- Laurie Kitchen, CA, FLMI
- Patricia K. London, CPA, FLMI
- Roberta McClellan, FLMI
- Martha A. Meyer, CPA, FLMI
- Steven D. Morris, CPA, FLMI

Textbook Review Panel

On behalf of LOMA, we particularly thank the members of the textbook review panel for *Financial Accounting and Reporting Requirements in Life Insurance Companies*. These individuals provided research materials, read and commented on the manuscript, answered many author queries, and provided ideas for ensuring the book's relevance to today's insurance companies. In short, this textbook would have been a very different product without their participation. Their critical judgment, diligence, patience, and technical expertise were essential to the book's accuracy and completeness. These members of the textbook development panel contributed personal time, shared their many years of professional experience and education, and guided the book's focus:

- Lucie Bergeron-Poulin, CMA, FLMI, ACS, Accountant, Industrial-Alliance Life Insurance Company

- Alan E. Close, CPA, FLMI, Associate Controller, Northwestern Mutual Life Insurance Company

- Stephen F. Dolan, CPA, FLMI, Senior Assistant Vice President, AMICA Life Insurance Company

- Michael J. Leick, FLMI, Senior Accountant, AEGON USA Realty Advisors, Inc.

- Sherrill A. Nobles, FLMI, ACS, Workflow Supervisor, AEGON USA

- Teresa O'Connor, CGA, Manager, Life Financial Reporting and Planning, Zurich Life Insurance Company of Canada

- Keith Rayburn, FLMI, CLU, ACS, AIRC, HIA, Senior Actuarial Assistant II, J.C. Penney Life Insurance Company

LOMA Staff and Consultants

All textbooks developed by LOMA are team projects. Many members of LOMA's Education & Training Division staff worked to create this textbook, as did other LOMA staff. The following individuals deserve special mention for the work they performed on this text.

Jena L. Kennedy, FLMI, ALHC, ACS, CLU, PAHM, Director, Education & Training, served as project manager. Susan Conant, FLMI, HIA, CEBS, PAHM, Education & Training, served as manuscript editor. Cynthia Mathis Henry, FLMI, ALHC, ACS, PAHM, Senior Associate, Examinations Department, served as examinations editor. Aurelia K. Hemphill, Administrative Assistant III, Education & Training, prepared the glossary and provided administrative support. Mamunah Carter and Marion Markus provided additional administrative support.

Audrey M. Hiers, Inventory and Product Sourcing Administrator, Education & Training, provided business support for production of the project. In LOMA's Production Department, Allison Ayers, Production Coordinator II, designed the cover and served as typesetter. Amy Souwan, Production Coordinator II/Print Coordinator, coordinated the printing of the book. LOMA consultant Iris F. Hartley, FLMI, ALHC, obtained permission for use of copyrighted material. Robert D. Land, FLMI, ACS, another LOMA consultant, copyedited the entire manuscript and prepared the index. Also, special thanks to Michelle Stone Weathers, ACS, Manager, Production Department, who moved the project through production.

From the staff of LOMA's Information Center, Olivia Blakemore, ACS, Technical Administrator, Information Center, along with Mallory Eldridge, Writer/Analyst, Information Center, and Janet Smith, Information Center Researcher, frequently assisted with research for the project.

And finally, thanks to William H. Rabel, Ph.D., FLMI, CLU, Senior Vice President, Education Division, for his encouragement and support throughout the text's development.

Elizabeth A. Mulligan, FLMI, ACS, ALHC, AIAA, PAHM
Atlanta, Georgia
2002

Introduction

Financial Accounting and Reporting Requirements in Life Insurance Companies has been designed for students who are preparing for the FLMI 361 examination, which is part of the Fellow, Life Management Institute (FLMI) designation program. Several features have been included in each chapter to help you organize your studies, reinforce your understanding of the materials, and prepare for the examination. As we describe each of these features, we give you suggestions for studying the material.

- **Learning Objectives.** The first page of each chapter contains a list of learning objectives to help you focus your studies. Before reading each chapter, review these learning objectives. Then, as you read the chapter, look for material that will help you meet the learning objectives.

- **Chapter Outline.** The first page of each chapter contains an outline of the chapter. Review this outline to gain an overview of the material that will be covered; then scan through the chapter to familiarize yourself with the presentation of the information. By looking at the headings and figures, you will get a preview of how the various subjects relate to each other.

- **Key Terms.** The key terms and concepts associated with insurance administration are reviewed and explained in this text. All of the important terminology introduced in this text is defined or explained when it is first used. Important terminology is highlighted with ***bold italic type*** when the term is first defined and is included in a list of key terms at the end of each chapter. All key terms also appear in a comprehensive glossary at the end of the book. As you read each chapter, pay special attention to these key terms.

- **Figures.** Figures appear throughout the text and are designed to illustrate or give examples of the text's discussions of selected important topics. Note that information contained in figures may be tested on FLMI Program examination.

- **Insights.** Insights appear throughout the text and are designed to amplify the text's descriptions of certain topics. These insights should help you get a better feel for the functional areas and activities involved in insurance administration. Information contained in insights may be tested on the examinations for this course and other LOMA courses.

- **Glossary.** A comprehensive glossary containing definitions of all key terms appears at the end of the book. Each glossary entry indicates in which chapter a key term is discussed. The glossary includes references to important equivalent terms, acronyms, and contrasting terms or concepts.

Using LOMA Study Aids

LOMA has prepared study aids designed to help students prepare for the Course FLMI 361 examination. LOMA recommends that you use all of the study aids available for this course. **Studies indicate that students who use LOMA study aids consistently perform significantly better on LOMA examinations than students who do not use these study aids.**

Using the Prep Pak for This Course

In addition to this book, LOMA's *Prep Pak for FLMI 361* is assigned reading for students preparing for the FLMI Program examination. Used along with this textbook, the Prep Pak will help you master the course material. The Prep Pak includes chapter review exercises, practice exam questions, a full-scale sample examination in both paper and electronic format, and answers to every question in the Prep Pak.

The *Prep Pak* may be revised periodically. To ensure that you are studying from the correct texts, check the current *LOMA Education and Training Catalog* for a description of the texts assigned for the examination for which you are preparing.

Finally, course instructors should know that LOMA has prepared an *Instructor's Kit for FLMI 361*, designed to help company instructors prepare to teach preparatory classes for the FLMI 361 examination.

Suggested LOMA Study Aids

Some students may find it helpful to undertake a quick review of material related to this course in LOMA *StepOne Series* publications:

- *Intro to Accounting* (1999) provides an overview of the concepts that you might encounter in studying *Financial Accounting and Reporting Requirements in Life Insurance.*

Chapter 1

Financial Statements and Reports

OBJECTIVES

After reading this chapter, you should be able to

⊕ Recognize and distinguish among the major types of accounts

⊕ Recognize the components and purposes of an insurer's key financial statements: the balance sheet, income statement, cash flow statement, and the statement of owners' equity

⊕ Identify whether specified transactions produce a cash inflow or a cash outflow

⊕ Classify transactions that affect an insurer's cash as one of three types of activities: operating activities, investing activities, or financing activities

⊕ Use the direct method or the indirect method to calculate net cash flows for a series of transactions

⊕ Distinguish between static and dynamic financial statements

⊕ Identify the relationships among the various financial statements

The accounting function provides a company with a structured way to maintain accurate, timely, and complete financial information about its business transactions and to satisfy financial reporting requirements. *Financial accounting* is the field of accounting that focuses primarily on reporting a company's financial information to meet the needs of the company's external users. The preparation of financial statements is the end product of financial accounting. *Financial statements* are standardized reports that summarize a company's major financial events and transactions.

The heading of every financial statement contains the following information: (1) the name of the company, (2) the name of the financial statement, and (3) the date of the financial statement or the accounting period covered by the financial statement. The heading of a financial statement shows whether the monetary amounts on a company's financial statements represent thousands, millions, or even billions of dollars. Companies usually round the reported amounts off to the nearest thousand or million.

Types of Accounts

The business transactions that a company records in its accounting system and reports on its financial statements typically involve five types of accounts: (1) assets, (2) liabilities, (3) owners' equity, (4) revenues, and (5) expenses. Figure 1-1 provides definitions and examples of each type of account.

Key Financial Statements

An insurer's financial statements contain the information that is believed to be essential for an external user to gain a general understanding of the insurer's financial condition, activities, and prospects. The following sections discuss an insurer's primary financial statements—the balance sheet, income statement, cash flow statement, and the statement of owners' equity.

Balance Sheet

The first three types of accounts depicted in Figure 1-1—assets, liabilities, and owners' equity—appear on a company's balance sheet. A

FIGURE 1-1. Types of Accounts.

ACCOUNT TYPE	DEFINITION	EXAMPLES
Assets	All items, generally of readily determined monetary value, that a company owns	Investments, cash, real estate
Liabilities	A company's monetary values for its current and future obligations	Current and future contractual benefits, accounts payable
Owners' equity	The owners' investment in a company	Common stock, capital, surplus
Revenues	The amounts earned from a company's core business operations	Premium income, investment income, fee income
Expenses	The amounts of one or more assets that a company uses to receive benefits, goods, or services	Agent commissions, contractual benefit expenses, administrative expenses

balance sheet is a financial statement that shows an insurer's financial condition or position as of a specified date. Every company compiles a balance sheet. The main purpose of the balance sheet is to measure, as of a specified date, the owners' wealth (owners' equity)—that is, what remains after subtracting what a company owes (liabilities) from what it owns (assets).

The **basic accounting equation**, sometimes called the *balance sheet equation*, presents the relationship among the three key account classifications on the balance sheet: assets, liabilities, and owners' equity. This relationship is generally expressed in the following equation:

Assets = Liabilities + Owners' equity

The basic accounting equation can also be expressed as follows:

Liabilities = Assets – Owners' equity

or

Owners' equity = Assets – Liabilities

A large portion of an insurer's assets consists of various investments, such as bonds, mortgages, stocks, and real estate. Most of the insurer's obligations—liabilities—consist of current and future contractual benefits and other obligations to customers. When you review a list of a company's assets, you see, in summary form, what the company purchased with the funds provided by the company's creditors, policyowners, and stockholders.

The monetary amounts listed on the balance sheet represent the company's summarized account balances on the date shown at the top of the balance sheet. In this context, a balance sheet is a *static report*—that is, a "snapshot" of a company's financial position—on a specified date. Note that the insurer's total assets equal its total liabilities and owners' equity. In other words, the two sides balance, giving this financial statement its name. Although a balance sheet contains valuable information, it does not reveal how or why a company purchased or sold particular items. Figure 1-2 shows an example of an insurer's balance sheet.

The balance sheet usually appears in one of two forms: the account form or the report form. In the **account form** of presentation, asset accounts appear on the left, and liability accounts and owners' equity accounts appear on the right. Most balance sheets appear in report form for financial reporting purposes. In the **report form** of presentation, asset, liability, and owners' equity accounts are presented sequentially. The balance sheet presented in Figure 1-2 illustrates the report form of presentation.

Income Statement

A company's revenues and expenses appear on the company's income statement. An **income statement** is a financial statement that (1) reports an insurer's revenues and expenses during a specified period and (2) indicates whether the insurer experienced net income or a net loss during the period. **Net income**, also known as *profit*, occurs if revenues for a reporting period exceed expenses for the period. A **net loss** occurs if expenses for a reporting period exceed the revenues for the period. Revenues are the first group of accounts listed on an insurer's income statement. Expenses, the second major account classification on the income statement, are a necessary part of doing business because a company cannot generate revenues without also incurring expenses.

Figure 1-3 shows an example of an insurer's income statement.

Unlike the balance sheet, which presents a company's financial position as of a single date, the income statement presents the company's revenues earned and expenses incurred during an accounting period. The income statement is a *dynamic report* in that it

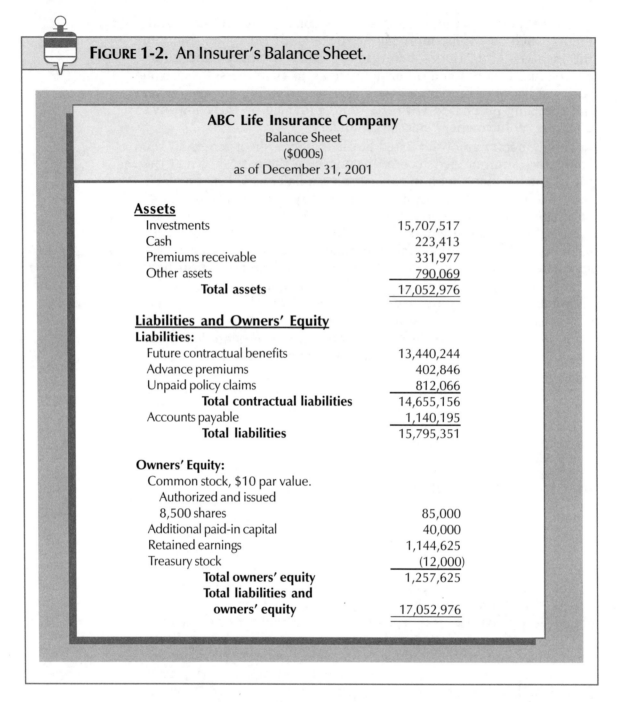

FIGURE 1-2. An Insurer's Balance Sheet.

ABC Life Insurance Company
Balance Sheet
($000s)
as of December 31, 2001

Assets

Investments	15,707,517
Cash	223,413
Premiums receivable	331,977
Other assets	790,069
Total assets	17,052,976

Liabilities and Owners' Equity

Liabilities:

Future contractual benefits	13,440,244
Advance premiums	402,846
Unpaid policy claims	812,066
Total contractual liabilities	14,655,156
Accounts payable	1,140,195
Total liabilities	15,795,351

Owners' Equity:

Common stock, $10 par value.	
Authorized and issued	
8,500 shares	85,000
Additional paid-in capital	40,000
Retained earnings	1,144,625
Treasury stock	(12,000)
Total owners' equity	1,257,625
Total liabilities and	
owners' equity	17,052,976

presents the movement or flow of business transactions during a specified accounting period.

Cash Flow Statement

A company's *cash flow statement* is a financial statement that provides information about the company's cash inflows and cash

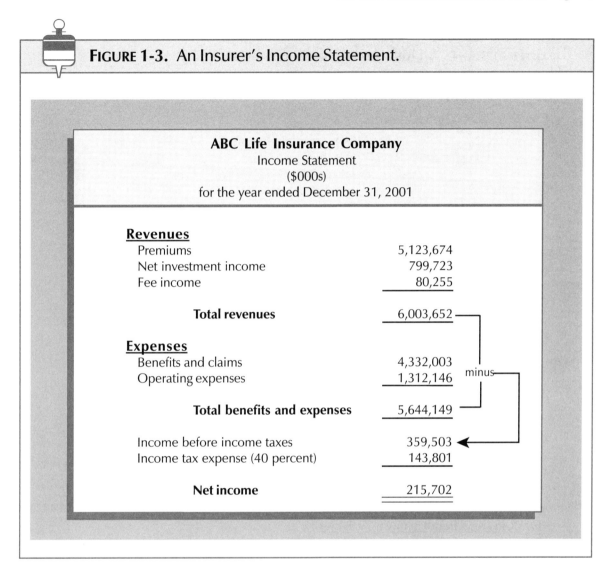

FIGURE 1-3. An Insurer's Income Statement.

ABC Life Insurance Company
Income Statement
($000s)
for the year ended December 31, 2001

Revenues

Premiums	5,123,674
Net investment income	799,723
Fee income	80,255
Total revenues	6,003,652

Expenses

Benefits and claims	4,332,003
Operating expenses	1,312,146
Total benefits and expenses	5,644,149

Income before income taxes	359,503
Income tax expense (40 percent)	143,801
Net income	215,702

minus

outflows during a specified period. In other words, a cash flow statement shows the activities associated with the changes between a company's cash at the beginning and the end of a specified accounting period. The primary purpose of a cash flow statement is to demonstrate how a company manages its cash over time. In this context, the cash flow statement is also a *dynamic report* of the company's financial performance.

Figure 1-4 shows an example of an insurer's cash flow statement.

Cash Inflows and Cash Outflows

In accounting terminology, a ***cash inflow*** is a source of funds and a ***cash outflow*** is a use of funds. Cash inflows include cash receipts, which is money that the insurer has received from policy premiums,

FIGURE 1-4. An Insurer's Cash Flow Statement.

ABC Life Insurance Company
Cash Flow Statement
($000s)
for the year ended December 31, 2001

Cash Flows from Operating Activities
  Cash receipts:

Premium income	$ 353,047	
Investment income	23,658	
Total cash receipts		376,705
Cash disbursements:		
Contractual benefits	$ (178,445)	
Policy dividends	(26,779)	
Operating expenses	(100,458)	
Income taxes	(27,549)	
Total cash disbursements		(333,231)
Net cash flows from operating activities		43,474

Cash Flows from Investing Activities

Sales of securities	$902,345	
Purchase of securities	(894,400)	
Purchase of equipment	(4,300)	
Net cash flows from investing activities		3,645

Cash Flows from Financing Activities

Cash payments for stockholder dividends	(22,709)	
Net cash flows used for financing activities		(22,709)
Net increase (decrease) in cash		24,410
Beginning period cash balance		35,750
Ending cash balance		60,160

investment income, and fee income. Cash outflows include cash disbursements, which is money that the insurer has paid for policy benefits, expenses associated with investment purchases, ongoing business expenses, and so on. Figure 1-5 includes examples of activities, with respect to balance sheet and income statement accounts,

FIGURE 1-5. Cash Inflows and Cash Outflows.

Cash inflows result from:

Activity/Transaction	Example
A decrease in an asset account	Selling an asset for cash
An increase in a liability account	Taking out a loan
An increase in an owners' equity account	Issuing common stock
An increase in a revenue account	Selling a life insurance policy

Cash outflows result from:

Activity/Transaction	Example
An increase in an asset account	Buying an asset for cash
A decrease in a liability account	Paying off a loan
A decrease in an owners' equity account	Retiring or repurchasing the company's own stock
A decrease in an expense account	Paying a utility bill

that result in cash inflows (sources of funds) or cash outflows (uses of funds).

For an accounting period, the net cash inflow or net cash outflow represents the ***net change in cash***—that is, the increase or decrease in cash. Theoretically, a company's net change in cash equals the difference between the cash balance as shown on any two consecutive balance sheets, such as the company's current and previous balance sheet. You can calculate a company's net cash flow during a specified period by subtracting the company's cash outflows from its cash inflows, as follows:

> **Cash inflows – Cash outflows =**
> **Net cash inflow (Net cash outflow)**

or

> **Sources of funds – Uses of funds = Net change in cash**

Changes in a company's cash flows occur as a result of three activities. These activities are defined and illustrated in Figure 1-6. Note that a company's investing activities include the company's purchase or sale of the stocks or bonds of other companies—which are asset accounts on the company's balance sheet. However, the company's issuance of its own stocks—which are owners' equity accounts, rather than asset accounts, on the company's balance sheet—are classified as financing activities.

If the cash inflows exceed the cash outflows for that activity, then the result for that activity is a net cash inflow. Conversely, if the cash outflows exceed the cash inflows, then the result is a net cash outflow. Figure 1-7 presents examples of net cash inflows and outflows and demonstrates the distinctions among the cash flows from operating, investing, and financing activities.

Direct Method and Indirect Method

To develop the cash flow statement, companies use one of two methods: (1) the direct method or (2) the indirect method. Cash flows from investing activities and financing activities are calculated similarly

FIGURE 1-6. Cash Flow Transactions by Type of Activity.

Type of Activity	Transactions Resulting in Cash Inflows	Transactions Resulting in Cash Outflows
Operating activities: Transactions that involve a company's major lines of business and that directly determine the company's net income	• Cash sales to customers • Receipts of interest and dividends • Fee income and other revenues	• Contractual benefit payments to policyowners and beneficiaries • Payments to employees and suppliers • Payments of interest to bondholders
Investing activities: Transactions that involve a company's purchase or sale of long-term assets and the lending of long-term funds to other companies	• Sales of bonds, mortgages, stocks, property, buildings, and other long-term assets • Receipts of principal and interest on loan repayments	• Purchases of bonds, mortgages, stocks, property, buildings, and other long-term assets • Disbursements of loans to borrowers
Financing activities: Transactions that involve borrowed funds and cash payments to or from a company's owners	• Issuances of common stock • Issuances of bonds or notes • Receipts of loan proceeds from creditors	• Payments of cash dividends to stockholders • Payments of principal and interest on debts such as bonds, loans, and notes

FIGURE 1-7. Examples of Net Cash Inflows and Outflows.

In 2001, the Gallant Life Insurance Company received $10 million in premium income and paid $8 million in contractual benefits. Gallant's 2001 cash flow statement would therefore include $2 million net cash inflows from operating activities, as follows:

$10 million cash inflows – $8 million cash outflows = $2 million net cash inflows from operating activities

Gallant also sold $150,000 of bonds and purchased $160,000 in mortgages during 2001. Gallant's cash flow statement would include $10,000 net cash outflows for investing activities, as follows:

$150,000 cash inflows – $160,000 cash outflows = $10,000 net cash outflows for investing activities

In addition to the above activities, Gallant paid $50,000 in cash dividends to stockholders during 2001. Gallant's cash flow statement would include $50,000 net cash outflows for financing activities, as follows:

$50,000 net cash outflows for financing activities

under both methods. The only difference between the two methods is the way that cash flows are calculated from operating activities. Figure 1-8 compares the direct method and indirect method of determining net cash from operating activities.

Statement of Owners' Equity

A company's **statement of owners' equity** is a financial statement that shows the changes that occurred in owners' equity during a specified period. Recall that the cash flow statement provides information about a company's change in cash between the company's current and previous balance sheet. Similarly, a company's statement of owners' equity provides information about the changes in the company's equity accounts between the current and previous balance sheets. Stock insurance companies are owned by their stockholders, whereas mutual insurance companies are owned by their customers. Stock insurers typically refer to this statement as the *statement of stockholders' equity*. Mutual insurers and fraternal insurers often prepare a similar statement, sometimes called the *statement of policyowners' equity* or the *statement of policyholders' equity*.

FIGURE 1-8. Cash Flows from Operating Activities: Direct Method and Indirect Method.

Cash Flow Statement
($000s)
for the year ended December 31, 2001

DIRECT METHOD

Cash Flows from Operating Activities

Cash receipts:

Premiums received	513,807	
Investment income received	65,292	
Total cash receipts		579,099

Cash disbursements:

Contractual benefits	(271,876)	
Policy dividends	(11,230)	
Operating expenses	(208,683)	
Income taxes	(39,168)	
Total cash disbursements		(530,957)
Net cash flows from operating activities		48,142

INDIRECT METHOD

Cash Flows from Operating Activities

Net income		58,753
Adjustments to reconcile net income		
to net cash from operating activities:		
Add: Increase in benefits payable	53,047	
Subtract: increase in accrued investment income	(51,220)	
Subtract: increase in deferred acquisition costs	(12,438)	
Total adjustments		(10,611)
Net cash flows from operating activities		48,142

The top portion of this figure shows the direct method. Note that this insurer presents operating cash receipts first, then subtracts operating cash disbursements to arrive at the amount of $48,142,000—the net cash inflow from operating activities. The bottom portion of this figure shows the indirect method, which begins with the net income reported on the insurer's income statement. The insurer makes adjustments to its net income to arrive indirectly at $48,142,000—again the net cash inflow from operating activities.

For stock insurers, events that cause owners' equity accounts to change include (1) an issuance of stock, (2) a purchase of treasury stock, (3) the retention of net income (retained earnings), (4) a payment of cash dividends on stock, and (5) an increase or a decrease in surplus. Because mutual insurers do not issue common stock, they typically experience changes in owners' equity as a result of changes in net income or surplus.

Figure 1-9 shows an example of a stock insurer's statement of owners' equity.

Financial Statement Integration

A company's financial statements are interrelated. For example, the income statement, the cash flow statement, and the statement of owners' equity are dynamic reports of a company's performance. They provide the critical links between the changes in two consecutive

FIGURE 1-9. An Insurer's Statement of Owners' Equity.

Statement of Owners' Equity ($000) for the year ended December 31, 2001		
Stock	Balance at beginning of year	20,000
	Capital stock issued during year	0
	Balance at end of year	20,000
Additional Paid-In Capital	Balance at beginning of year	435,000
	Change during year	0
	Balance at end of year	435,000
Treasury Stock	Balance at beginning of year	0
	Purchases during year	(10,000)
	Balance at end of year	(10,000)
Net Unrealized Gains (Losses)	Balance at beginning of year	(126,290)
	Change during year	334,628
	Balance at end of year	208,338
Retained Earnings	Balance at beginning of year	2,774,350
	Net income (loss)	201,865
	Dividends paid	(165,750)
	Balance at end of year	2,810,465
Total owners' equity at end of year		3,463,803

balance sheets, which are static reports of the company's financial condition. For example, net income on a company's income statement directly affects the amount of the company's owners' equity. Figure 1-10 shows the relationship between static and dynamic financial statements.

Changes in an insurer's revenues, expenses, or net income (net loss) ultimately affect the insurer's balance sheet. An increase in an insurer's revenues typically increases its assets. For example, when a policyowner pays a policy premium or the insurer receives investment income, these transactions not only increase an insurer's revenues, but also its cash, which is an asset account. In contrast, an increase in an insurer's expenses typically decreases the insurer's assets. Similarly, when an insurer pays contractual benefits or agent commissions (both are expenses), the insurer's cash account (an asset) decreases. Further, the amount of a company's net income or net loss ultimately is reflected in the owners' equity portion of the company's balance sheet.

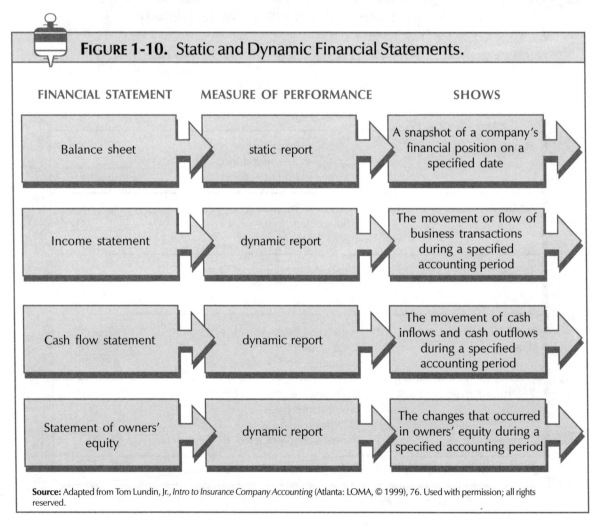

FIGURE 1-10. Static and Dynamic Financial Statements.

FINANCIAL STATEMENT	MEASURE OF PERFORMANCE	SHOWS
Balance sheet	static report	A snapshot of a company's financial position on a specified date
Income statement	dynamic report	The movement or flow of business transactions during a specified accounting period
Cash flow statement	dynamic report	The movement of cash inflows and cash outflows during a specified accounting period
Statement of owners' equity	dynamic report	The changes that occurred in owners' equity during a specified accounting period

Source: Adapted from Tom Lundin, Jr., *Intro to Insurance Company Accounting* (Atlanta: LOMA, © 1999), 76. Used with permission; all rights reserved.

The Annual Report

All stock insurers and many mutual and fraternal insurers develop an annual report to provide financial information to stockholders and investors (if a stock company), policyowners, and others. Generally, an **annual report** is a document that a company's management sends to interested parties to report on the company's financial performance during the past year. A company's annual report includes the company's key financial statements. All companies that offer shares of their own stock for sale on a public stock exchange must publish an annual report for their stockholders. Whether presented in an annual report or elsewhere, these financial statements provide information for external parties who are interested in a company's financial condition.

The heart of an insurer's annual report consists of the insurer's key financial statements—the balance sheet, income statement, cash flow statement, and statement of owners' equity. Besides financial statements, an insurer's annual report includes the

- Letter to stockholders and financial highlights

- Notes and supplementary information

- Management discussion and analysis of financial condition and results of operations (MD&A)

- Auditor's report

The financial statements contained in the annual report of a stock insurer in the United States are prepared using generally accepted accounting principles for companies operating in the United States. The annual report of an insurer in Canada is prepared according to generally accepted accounting principles for companies operating in Canada. **Generally accepted accounting principles (GAAP)** are a set of financial accounting standards that all publicly traded companies in the United States and all companies in Canada follow when preparing their financial statements.

The Annual Statement and the Annual Return

The **Annual Statement** is a financial report that every insurer in the United States must file annually, as well as on a quarterly basis, with the National Association of Insurance Commissioners (NAIC) and the insurance regulatory organization in each state in which the insurer conducts business. ***Statutory accounting practices*** are accounting standards that all life insurers in the United States must follow when preparing the Annual Statement.

The Canadian equivalent of the U.S. Annual Statement is the ***Annual Return***, which each insurer in Canada must file with the Office of the Superintendent of Financial Institutions (OSFI) and with the insurance regulatory organization in each province in which the insurer conducts business. Canadian GAAP is the accounting standard used to prepare the Annual Return.

Textbook Overview

This textbook provides an overview of financial accounting and financial reporting requirements for life insurance companies in the United States and Canada. Below is a list of topics covered in *Financial Accounting and Reporting Requirements in Life Insurance Companies:*

- Financial statements

- Invested assets

- Assets other than invested assets

- Reserves

- Liabilities other than reserves

- Capital and surplus

- Revenues

- Expenses

- Financial ratio analysis

- Regulatory monitoring of life insurance companies

Key Terms and Concepts

financial accounting
financial statements
assets
liabilities

owners' equity
revenues
expenses
balance sheet

Key Terms and Concepts (*continued*)

basic accounting equation
account form
report form
income statement
net income
net loss
cash flow statement
cash inflow
cash outflow
net change in cash

operating activities
investing activities
financing activities
statement of owners' equity
annual report
generally accepted accounting
   principles (GAAP)
Annual Statement
statutory accounting practices
Annual Return

Chapter 2

Accounting for Invested Assets

OBJECTIVES

After reading this chapter, you should be able to

- Describe the five key account classifications

- Describe several asset valuation methods

- Recognize examples of a life insurance company's typical short-term assets

- Demonstrate an understanding of accounting entries for the purchase and sale of a bond or stock

- Differentiate between common stock and preferred stock

Recall from Chapter 1 that assets are all items, generally of readily determined monetary value, that a company owns. This chapter describes accounting for invested assets. We begin with an overview of asset classification. We briefly discuss asset valuation. We also describe how an insurer accounts for and reports typical asset transactions.

Asset Characteristics

An insurer uses the income generated by its assets to support its obligations for current and future contractual benefits. On the balance sheet, insurers typically list their securities first, followed by short-term assets, then long-term assets and other assets. **Securities** are financial agreements representing evidence of the right to collect repayment of a loan, ownership of an asset, or the legal right to purchase or sell ownership of an asset. Examples of securities include bonds, mortgages, and stock, which we discuss in this chapter. To organize a company's assets into a meaningful order on the balance sheet, assets are assigned to various classifications, as shown in Figure 2-1. Note that a specified asset can be assigned to several different classifications—for example, a short-term asset is either tangible or intangible. The following sections discuss these different ways of classifying assets: by their term to maturity, as tangible or intangible, and as admitted or nonadmitted.

Term to Maturity

Term to maturity refers to the amount of time that passes before an asset can be converted to cash for an approximation of its value. For investments in the United States, **short term** is defined as covering less than one year, **intermediate term** is typically defined as covering from one to 10 years, and **long term** is typically defined as any period greater than 10 years. Usage differs somewhat within the United States concerning the length of intermediate term and long term, although the length of short term is consistently viewed as being less than one year. Also, usage differs in Canada, where *short term* is consistently defined as covering from zero to six years, *intermediate term* is consistently defined as covering from more than six years to 10 years, and *long term* is consistently defined as any period greater than 10 years.

Because short-term assets have a high degree of liquidity, they are also sometimes referred to as *liquid assets*. **Liquidity** refers to the

FIGURE 2-1. Classifications of Insurers' Assets.

Asset Type	Short-term also called *current assets*, are assets that a company expects to convert to cash within one year.	Long-term also called *noncurrent assets*, are assets that a company expects to retain for more than one year.	Tangible are assets that have physical form.	Intangible are assets that represent ownership of a legal right or another nonphysical resource.	Debt are assets that represent the investor's loan of funds to the debt issuer in return for the promised repayment of principal and payment of interest.	Equity are assets that represent the investor's ownership or share of ownership in an asset such as a business or property.
Common Stocks	No	Yes	No	Yes	No	Yes
Bonds	No	Yes	No	Yes	Yes	No
Mortgages	No	Yes	No	Yes	Yes	No
Policy Loans	No	Yes	No	Yes	Yes	No
Real Estate	No	Yes	Yes	No	No	Yes
Cash	Yes	No	Yes	No	No	Yes

ease with which an asset can be converted into cash for an approximation of its true value. Short-term assets include cash and cash equivalents. **Cash** is the amount of currency on hand or on deposit at an insurer's bank. **Cash equivalents** are short-term assets that are not cash, but typically can be converted to cash within 90 days with little or no risk of losing value. **Treasury bills**, which are short-term assets issued and guaranteed by the U.S. government, are a specific type of cash equivalent.

Unlike short-term assets, long-term assets are significantly less liquid than short-term assets. Accordingly, insurers typically do not use long-term assets as a source of ready cash. Long-term government bonds, corporate bonds, stocks, real estate, and mortgages are examples of an insurer's long-term assets.

Tangible Assets and Intangible Assets

Assets may also be tangible or intangible. Tangible assets have physical form. Intangible assets represent ownership of a legal right or another nonphysical resource. Examples of tangible assets include cash, real estate, automobiles, collectibles, equipment, and machinery. Important examples of intangible assets are securities, patents, copyrights, computer software, leases, and licenses.

Admitted Assets and Nonadmitted Assets

To comply with statutory reporting requirements, life insurance companies in the United States must also classify their assets as admitted assets and nonadmitted assets for the Annual Statement. Under statutory accounting practices, an insurer's assets may be (1) entirely admitted, (2) partially admitted, or (3) entirely nonadmitted. The purpose of differentiating between admitted assets and non-admitted assets is to enable state insurance regulators to readily determine an insurer's assets that are available to meet policyowner obligations.

Admitted assets are assets whose full value is reported on the Assets page of the U.S. Annual Statement. Examples of admitted assets include cash and cash equivalents and most invested assets. *Partially admitted assets* are assets for which only a portion of their monetary value is reported on the Assets page of the U.S. Annual Statement. Partially admitted assets include invested assets reduced by any amount that exceeds statutory investment limitations. *Nonadmitted assets* are assets that are accorded no value on the Assets page of the U.S. Annual Statement. Examples of nonadmitted assets include an insurer's office furniture and supplies. Figure 2-2 summarizes some typical admitted assets and nonadmitted assets.

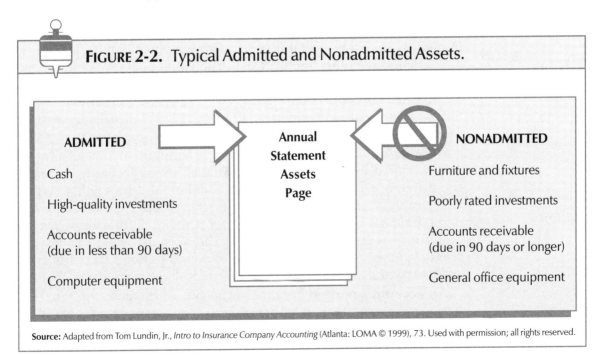

FIGURE 2-2. Typical Admitted and Nonadmitted Assets.

ADMITTED	Annual Statement Assets Page	NONADMITTED
Cash		Furniture and fixtures
High-quality investments		Poorly rated investments
Accounts receivable (due in less than 90 days)		Accounts receivable (due in 90 days or longer)
Computer equipment		General office equipment

Source: Adapted from Tom Lundin, Jr., *Intro to Insurance Company Accounting* (Atlanta: LOMA © 1999), 73. Used with permission; all rights reserved.

Asset Valuation

Insurers use several methods of asset valuation. **Valuation** is the process of calculating the monetary value of an insurer's assets, liabilities, and owners' equity. Insurance regulators typically specify the valuation methods insurers must use for different types of assets. For example, under statutory accounting practices, insurers in the United States generally report the current market value of their common stock investments and report the amortized cost of their bond investments. Insurers in Canada report bonds at amortized cost and stocks according to the moving average market method, which we describe later in this chapter. Figure 2-3 describes the common methods used to value an insurer's assets.

Accounting Entries

Companies use accounting entries to record their financial transactions. An **accounting entry** is a record of a financial transaction that (1) includes at least one debit and one credit and (2) shows the monetary value of the transaction on a specified date. In an accounting entry, the total of the debits must always equal exactly the total of the credits.

A **debit**, a type of monetary change made to an account, increases the value of asset accounts and expense accounts and decreases the value of liability accounts, owners' equity accounts, and revenue accounts. A **credit**, a type of monetary change made to an account, increases the value of liability accounts, owners' equity accounts, and revenue accounts and decreases the value of asset accounts and expense accounts. In our text examples, so that you may more easily distinguish debits from credits, we use the commonly accepted format of presenting debits first and to the left, followed by credits, indented to the right.

An account's balance is the monetary amount in the account as of a specified date. To obtain the balance in an account, calculate the difference between the account's debits and its credits. When an account's debits exceed its credits, the account is said to have a *debit balance* or a normal balance of a debit. Similarly, when an account's credits exceed its debits, the account is said to have a *credit balance* or a normal balance of a credit. Some accounts typically carry a debit balance; others usually have a credit balance.

An account's **normal balance** is the side of the account, whether debit or credit, to which increases to the account are recorded.

FIGURE 2-3. Asset Valuation.

An asset's **historical cost** is the purchase price originally paid for the asset.

The **book value** of an asset is the asset's original cost, adjusted for capitalized acquisition costs, accumulated depreciation, and other specified amounts. On the date of purchase, an asset's historical cost equals its book value.

Current market value, also called *fair market value*, is the price at which the asset can be sold under current economic conditions. The current market value of most assets fluctuates over time and may vary considerably from both its historical cost and its amortized cost.

An asset's **amortized cost** is the asset's historical cost, less any adjustment, such as *depreciation* or *amortization*, to the asset's book value.

Depreciation is the accounting process of allocating (spreading) the cost of an asset over the asset's estimated useful life. Depreciation typically applies to an insurer's long-term, tangible assets such as buildings.

Amortization is the accounting process by which an insurer periodically and systematically increases or decreases the original cost of an investment to its ultimate value at maturity. Amortization typically applies to an insurer's long-term, intangible assets such as bonds and mortgages.

The **lower of cost or market (LCM) rule** defines a bond's monetary value as either its amortized cost or its current market value, whichever is lower. Under statutory accounting, insurers in the United States report specified bond values according to the LCM rule.

Under U.S. GAAP, furniture and office equipment are reported as assets on an insurance company's balance sheet at their net book value. An asset's **net book value** is the asset's historical cost less accumulated depreciation only. An asset's net book value may be greater than its current market value.

Accounts that are increased by debits typically have a debit balance at the end of an accounting period. Accounts that are increased by credits typically have a credit balance at the end of an accounting period. Thus, asset accounts and expense accounts normally have a debit balance, whereas liability accounts, owners' equity accounts, and revenue accounts normally have a credit balance. Figure 2-4 summarizes the normal account balances for five key account classifications.

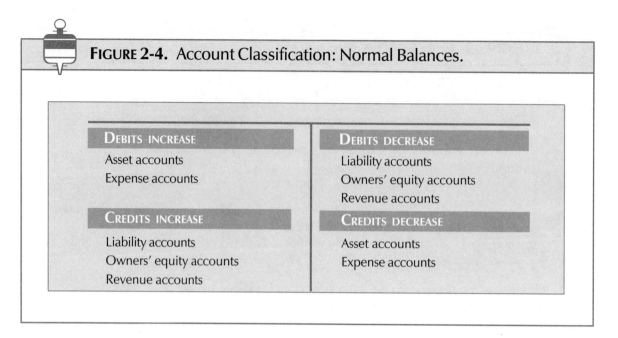

FIGURE 2-4. Account Classification: Normal Balances.

DEBITS INCREASE	DEBITS DECREASE
Asset accounts	Liability accounts
Expense accounts	Owners' equity accounts
	Revenue accounts

CREDITS INCREASE	CREDITS DECREASE
Liability accounts	Asset accounts
Owners' equity accounts	Expense accounts
Revenue accounts	

Accounting for Asset Transactions

A company records the purchase of an asset by debiting an asset account and crediting either another asset account or a liability account, or both, depending on how the company pays for the asset. Similarly, the company records the sale of an asset by crediting the asset account and debiting another asset account or liability account, or both, depending on how the company receives payment for the asset. Figure 2-5 shows several sample accounting entries to record the purchase and sale of an asset. Keep these general transactions in mind as we discuss the accounting aspects of specific assets in the following sections. Note, however, that insurers generally purchase and sell *invested* assets for cash, not on account.

Invested Assets

Before we discuss accounting for specific invested assets, we will first examine the terminology of investments. **Invested assets**, also called *investments*, consist primarily of the debt securities, equity securities, and derivative securities purchased by an insurer to generate earnings. **Investing** refers to employing a principal sum of money to generate earnings. In a financial sense, investing usually

FIGURE 2-5. Recording Asset Purchases and Sales.

PURCHASE REAL ESTATE FOR CASH

      Real Estate .... $$$
           Cash .... $$$
      To record the purchase of real estate for cash.

The purchase of real estate increased the value of the insurer's *Real Estate* account by a specified monetary amount, and the insurer's *Cash* account—another asset account—decreased by the same amount. Note that this transaction does not change the value of the insurer's total assets nor does it affect any of the insurer's liability accounts or owners' equity accounts.

PURCHASE REAL ESTATE ON ACCOUNT

      Real Estate .... $$$
           Accounts Payable—Real Estate .... $$$
      To record the purchase of real estate on account.

In this transaction, the insurer purchased real estate on account. To purchase an asset ***on account*** means that the insurer incurs a liability, which the insurer promises to pay to the seller in the future. An ***account payable*** is a liability account that represents a promise of payment by the insurer to another party. A liability account normally has a credit balance, so a credit is used to record an increase in the value of a liability. Here, the insurer's total assets increased by the value of the purchased asset and the insurer's total liabilities increased by the same amount.

PURCHASE REAL ESTATE ON ACCOUNT, WITH CASH DOWN PAYMENT

      Real Estate .... $$$
           Cash .... $
           Accounts Payable—Real Estate .... $$
      To record the purchase of real estate on account, with a cash down payment.

The above transaction in effect combines the first two transactions: the insurer purchases real estate by making a cash down payment and incurring the remaining amount as a liability to be paid in the future. Because each accounting entry must have an equal monetary value for its debits and its credits, the sum of the debits—the monetary amount assigned to the *Real Estate* account—must equal the sum of the credits—*Cash* plus *Accounts Payable—Real Estate*. The monetary value of the real estate that the insurer reports on its balance sheet as of a specified date is the difference between the debits and credits in the *Real Estate* account through that date.

SELL REAL ESTATE FOR CASH

      Cash .... $$$
           Real Estate .... $$$
      To record the sale of real estate for cash.

To record the sale of an asset, an insurer would in effect reverse the accounting entry made when purchasing the asset for cash.

SELL REAL ESTATE ON ACCOUNT

      Accounts Receivable—Real Estate .... $$$
           Real Estate .... $$$
      To record the sale of real estate on account.

In this case, the insurer sold the real estate and, instead of cash, received an asset known as *Accounts Receivable—Real Estate*. An ***account receivable*** is a contractual promise to pay the seller. In this example, the insurer is the seller.

SELL REAL ESTATE ON ACCOUNT, WITH CASH DOWN PAYMENT

      Cash .... $
      Accounts Receivable—Real Estate .... $$
           Real Estate .... $$$
      To record the sale of real estate on account, with a cash down payment.

The sale of real estate included a cash down payment and the balance due on account.

involves using a principal sum of money to purchase assets or placing a sum on deposit. An investment *portfolio* is a collection of various assets assembled for the purpose of meeting a defined set of investment goals. The assets in a portfolio can be classified according to whether they represent debt securities, equity securities, or derivative securities. Insurance companies hold a much greater monetary share of their assets in debt securities than in equity securities or derivative securities. We discuss derivative securities in Chapter 3.

Important examples of debt securities are bonds and mortgages. A *bond* is a debt security issued by a borrower. In a bond certificate, the bond issuer promises to (1) pay a stated rate of interest according to a specified schedule and (2) repay the borrowed sum by a specified maturity date. A *mortgage* is a loan secured by a pledge of specified real property. In this context, the insurer is the purchaser of the bond or mortgage. By purchasing debt securities, the insurer can generally expect to receive a stated rate of return.

The stock of another company that an insurer purchases is an important example of an equity security. A *stock* is an asset that represents a stockholder's ownership interest in a company. Stock is sold in shares, and anyone who owns shares of stock in a company is a *stockholder* or *shareholder*.

Insurers must be reasonably certain that their investments provide the income needed for their current and future obligations. Investment goals usually focus on factors such as risk and return. In investing, a *risk* is the possibility that an investor will fail to earn an expected return or will lose all or part of an investment. A *return* is the reward an investor hopes to receive for taking a risk. Returns can take the form of interest, rent, price appreciation, or dividends, and may be expressed in terms of a percentage of the principal. A return expressed as a percentage relative to the invested principal is called a *rate of return*. As risk goes up, return must also go up to justify the risk assumed. As risk goes down, return goes down. This direct relationship between risk and return is called the *risk-return trade-off*, and it applies to all types of investments and to all types of risk.

The following sections discuss how insurance companies account for and report the assets in their investment portfolios.

Bonds

Bonds are usually issued by corporations or governments. Bonds issued by corporations are called *corporate bonds*, whereas those issued by governments—including federal, state, provincial, county, city, and other local governments—are called *government bonds*.

By far the largest category of life insurance company assets is corporate bonds, but insurance companies also invest a considerable amount of money in government bonds.

Insurers typically maintain detailed accounting records—including the principal, interest rate, interest payment dates, name of the bond issuer, issue date, and maturity date—for each bond that they own. They also report summary information about their bond investments in their financial statements under U.S. GAAP, Canadian GAAP, and U.S. statutory accounting practices. Bonds have a special terminology, which is presented in Figure 2-6 and discussed in the following sections.

Bonds produce income to the bondholder in the form of payments of interest. Typically, the bond issuer pays the interest semiannually to the bondholder. For example, the owner of a $1,000 par value bond that pays an annual interest rate of 10 percent will receive a

FIGURE 2-6. Bond Terminology.

Term	Definition
Bond issuer	The entity that sells the bond to raise money
Bondholder	The owner of a bond
Bond principal	Also called *par value, face amount, maturity value,* or *face value,* the amount of money originally borrowed; the designated legal monetary value assigned to each bond—generally $1,000
Stated rate	The rate of interest specified on the bond certificate
Interest payment	The monetary amount of income that a bond issuer pays on the bond to the bondholder
Maturity date	The date on which the bond issuer must repay to the bondholder the amount originally borrowed
Secured bond	A bond in which the issuer pledges something of value to guarantee the safety of the bondholder's investment
Collateral	Something of value, usually a portion of the bond issuer's assets, which the bondholder will receive if the bond issuer fails to make the contracted interest and principal payments on the bond
Debenture	An unsecured corporate bond

$50 interest payment twice each year, calculated as follows: $1,000 par value × 10 percent rate of interest ÷ 2 payments each year.

A bond has a fixed maturity period, which generally extends from two to 30 years after the issue date. Life insurers generally invest in intermediate- and long-term bonds. When a bond is first sold, the selling price is the bond's current market value, although this price fluctuates thereafter according to competitive market forces. Fluctuations in a bond's price are generally inversely related to fluctuations in market interest rates. In other words, if market interest rates rise, a bond's price falls. If market interest rates fall, a bond's price rises. Thus, besides earning interest on a bond's principal, a bondholder can also realize a profit from the sale of a bond, if the bond sells for a price higher than its purchase price. The inverse relationship between the market value for bonds and the level of market interest rates results from competitive forces in the market for bonds, as shown in Insight 2-1.

The following sections discuss how insurance companies account for and report their transactions associated with bond investments.

Bond Purchases and Sales

When an insurer purchases a bond, the insurer typically records the bond's value at its cost—that is, the price that the insurer paid for the bond—whether or not that amount matches the bond principal. An insurer may purchase a bond at a price that differs from the bond's par value. An insurer may also sell a bond that it owns at a price that differs from the bond's principal or original purchase price.

The sale of a bond may result in a capital gain or capital loss. A *capital gain* is the amount by which the selling price of an asset exceeds its purchase price, and a *capital loss* is the amount by which the purchase price of an asset exceeds its selling price. Capital gains

---

 Insight 2-1. **Bond Prices and Market Interest Rates.**

Acme Corporation issued a bond at $1,000 with a stated interest rate of 5 percent. If market interest rates later were to fall to 3 percent, Acme, as the bond issuer, would still be obligated to pay interest at a rate of 5 percent. Further suppose that the Frieze Life Insurance Company owns a block of these Acme 5 percent bonds. With market interest rates at 3 percent, Frieze would then demand a bond price higher than $1,000, because the Acme bond's high stated rate of interest would make it a premium buy in a market where bonds of comparable quality no longer offered a 5 percent interest rate. Thus, Frieze would demand a bond price higher than the bond's principal.

Conversely, if interest rates were later to rise to 8 percent, then Frieze, as the bond's owner, would face a market bond price lower than the bond's principal. Market forces ensure that the market price and the stated rate of interest will produce a rate of investment return equal to the current market interest rate on bonds of similar quality.

and losses are categorized in the United States as either realized or unrealized. In the United States, a *realized* capital gain or loss would generally result only from the actual sale of a bond or other asset. The **realized gain (loss)** from the sale of an asset is the difference between that asset's net sales proceeds and its book value. Unlike a realized gain (loss), an *unrealized* gain (loss) does not result from the actual sale of an asset. An **unrealized gain (loss)** is the difference between the book value of an invested asset and its admitted value under statutory accounting practices or its current market value under GAAP.

Bond Interest

Bond interest is typically paid on a semiannual basis. If an insurer buys a bond between interest payment dates, the insurer receives accrued income as part of the next interest payment, even though the bond's seller earned this interest. In the context of bond interest income, *accrued income* is the amount of interest that has been earned on a bond, but is not yet payable to the bondholder as of the financial reporting date. To compensate the seller for this lost interest, the bond's purchase price must include an amount equal to the accrued interest income as of the date of purchase. Suppose an insurer purchases a $1,000 bond at par with a 10 percent interest rate and semiannual payments—that is, two interest payments per year of $50 each—with $20 accrued interest income as of the purchase date. The insurer's purchase price is $1,020, calculated as follows:

> **$1,000 purchase price + $20 accrued income = $1,020**

The insurer records the accrued interest as an asset—specifically an account receivable—as shown in the following accounting entry. The insurer expects to receive the full amount of the bond interest—$50 in our example—when the next semiannual interest payment is made.

> **Bonds**... **1,000**
> **Investment Income Due and Accrued** **20**
>   **Cash**... **1,020**
>
> **To record the purchase of bonds with accrued bond interest income.**

Note that some insurers record the $20 purchased interest as a charge against investment income. Upon receipt of this interest payment, the insurer would record the following accounting entry:

Cash... 50	
Investment Income Due and Accrued 20	
Bond Interest Income................................. 30	
To record accrued and received bond interest income.	

Keep in mind that *Investment Income Due and Accrued* is an asset account, but *Bond Interest Income* is a revenue account. For financial reporting purposes, insurers report accrued revenues on the balance sheet and revenues on the income statement under both GAAP and statutory accounting practices.

Bond Discounts and Bond Premiums

Because of the inverse relationship between interest rates and bond prices, a bond's purchase price often differs from its principal, typically $1,000. Thus, a bond's current market value does not necessarily equal the bond's principal. When a bond's current market value is greater than the bond's principal, the excess of the price over the principal is termed a **premium**. When a bond's current market value is less than the bond's principal, the difference between the current market value and the principal is a **discount**. Generally, a bond will sell at a discount—that is, less than $1,000—if market interest rates are higher than the bond's stated interest rate and will sell at a premium—that is, greater than $1,000—if market interest rates are lower than the bond's stated interest rate.

Note that the annual amount of interest paid on a bond is a stated rate of return, regardless of the actual price paid for the bond. If the purchase price differs from the bond's principal, then the actual rate of return—known as the **effective rate of return** or *effective yield*—on the amount paid for the bond will differ from the stated rate of return. Generally, the effective rate of return on a bond is higher than the stated rate of return for a bond purchased at a discount and lower than the stated rate of return for a bond purchased at a premium. Suppose an insurer purchases a 10 percent, $1,000 bond for $1,100, and the bond matures in one year. In this case, the insurer's effective rate of return is 9.1 percent—that is, lower than the 10 percent stated rate—calculated as follows:

$$\text{\$100 bond interest} \div \text{\$1,100 purchase price}$$

Mortgages

Most insurers invest in mortgages primarily through mortgage-backed bonds, known as **collateralized mortgage obligations (CMOs)**, which are secured by a pool of residential mortgage loans. Mortgages and CMOs appeal to insurers because these debt securities generally return a predictable stream of cash flows because they provide (1) monthly debt repayment schedules; and (2) a minimum, often fixed rate of return. For U.S. Annual Statement purposes, insurers typically account for CMOs in the same manner as they report their bond investments. Insurers in Canada disclose both the book value and the current market value of their mortgages in the Annual Return.

Although the purchase or sale of a bond at a discount or premium is common, insurers seldom purchase mortgages at a premium or discount. Mortgage lenders, including insurers, sometimes require borrowers to pay additional amounts, which are recorded in a specific liability account, known as an escrow account. An **escrow account** is a trust account used to pay property maintenance expenses, property taxes, and other expenses related to a mortgaged property. Many lenders establish escrow accounts to ensure that the property is maintained at some minimum level. The insurer debits *Cash* and credits the *Escrow—Property X* account upon receiving escrow funds from the borrower. Escrow accounts are typically not used for bond investments.

When the insurer pays property taxes or other property expenses related to the mortgaged property, the insurer debits the escrow account, credits the appropriate property expense account, and credits *Cash*. The amount to be placed in escrow remains the same each month until a change in taxes, insurance premiums, or other expenses necessitates a change. Because these amounts are accounted for separately from the principal and interest payments on the mortgage loan, escrow account transactions do not affect the outstanding principal and interest payments on the mortgage.

Stocks

Recall that the purchased stock of other companies is considered an equity security to the insurer, which is the stockholder is this context. Like bonds, stock investments have a special terminology, which is presented in Figure 2-7. The two major classes of stock are common stock and preferred stock. Of these two classes, common stock comprises the majority of all stock issued.

Statutes limit the percentage of stocks that insurers can hold in the general account. Thus, equity securities comprise a much smaller portion of an insurer's investment portfolio than do bonds and other debt securities. However, an insurer's investments in equity securities can represent a large monetary amount. The following sections discuss accounting for stocks from the stockholder's point of view,

FIGURE 2-7. Stock Terminology.

Term	Definition
Par value of stock	In the context of stock, the designated legal value assigned to each outstanding share of common stock
Common stock	A unit of ownership that usually entitles the owner to (1) vote on the selection of directors and on other important company matters and (2) receive dividends on the stock
Preferred stock	A unit of ownership that typically does not carry the voting rights of common stock, but does carry a stated dividend rate or monetary amount that has a priority over that of dividends on common stock
Dividend on stock	A share of a company's earnings that the company pays to its stockholders
Cash dividend on stock	A cash payment that a company distributes periodically to the owners of its preferred stock and common stock
Stock dividend	A dividend that a company pays, in the form of additional shares of company stock, to its stockholders

with the assumption that an insurance company is the stockholder. In Chapter 6, we discuss accounting for stocks when the insurer issues its own stock.

Stock Purchases and Sales

Accounting for the purchase and sale of stock held for investment purposes is similar to that for the purchase and sale of bonds. Insurers record their stock purchases at cost. Insurers in the United States report the current market value per share of each stock they own on their December 31 balance sheet. The amount of any change in the market value of a stock is recorded as an unrealized gain or loss on that stock. On the U.S. Annual Statement, most common stock is reported at current market value as of the statement date, and most preferred stock is reported at cost, not to exceed fair value. The insurer also reports an unrealized loss for the difference between the stock's book value and its current market value. Figure 2-8 presents some transactions associated with owning stock.

FIGURE 2-8. Stock Transactions.

PURCHASE STOCK XYZ FOR CASH

Suppose the Stalwart Life Insurance Company purchases 100 shares of Stock XYZ for $95 per share. For the purposes of our discussion, we will ignore the effects of transactions costs, such as brokerage commissions. Stalwart records the transaction by debiting the cost of the stock to the *Stock XYZ* account and crediting *Cash* for the same amount. The accounting entry is as follows:

Stock XYZ 9,500
            Cash 9,500

To record the purchase of Stock XYZ.

When Stalwart sells the stock, the accounting entry includes a debit to *Cash* for the amount of cash received, which is typically the number of shares sold times the market price per share at the time of sale. If Stalwart sells the stock for $8,000, then the accounting entry is

Cash 8,000
Loss on Sale of Stock XYZ 1,500
            Stock XYZ 9,500

To record the sale of Stock XYZ at a loss.

Suppose Stalwart instead sells Stock XYZ for $12,000. The accounting entry to record the stock sale is

Cash 12,000
            Stock XYZ 9,500
            Gain on Sale of Stock XYZ 2,500

To record the sale of Stock XYZ at a gain.

CANADIAN PRACTICES

For Annual Return purposes, insurers in Canada credit *Deferred Realized Gains (Losses)* instead of *Gain on Sale of Stock*, then amortize a percentage of the gain on the income statement. In addition, insurers in Canada debit *Deferred Realized Gains (Losses)* instead of *Loss on Sale of Stock* in the above accounting entries, then amortize a designated percentage of the *Deferred Realized Gain (Loss)* into income.

Insurers in Canada also use the ***moving average market method*** to systematically adjust unrealized gains or losses that result from changes in the current market value of equity investments over a period of years. Insurance companies that conduct business in Canada report both the book value and the current market value of a stock in the Annual Return. The difference between the stock's book value and its current market value is amortized (spread) over time into the insurer's income on the income statement. The moving average market method is an attempt to measure long-term investment performance by minimizing the effects of volatile market values for invested assets in the short term.

Cash Dividends

Cash dividends on common stock usually are expressed as an annual monetary amount per share. Cash dividends on preferred stock typically are expressed as a percentage of par value per share. Dividends are typically paid quarterly. Suppose a common stock has an annual cash dividend of $1. An insurer that owns 1,000 shares of common stock will receive a cash dividend of $250 each quarter on this stock—the annual dividend is $1,000—calculated as shown: 1,000 shares × $1 × ¼. In another example, a preferred stock that has a par value of $10 may have a cash dividend expressed as 10 percent of its par value, resulting in an annual dividend of $1 per share.

A typical accounting entry to record the receipt of cash dividends is a debit to *Cash*, an asset account, and a credit to a revenue account such as *Dividend Income—Common Stock* or *Dividend Income— Preferred Stock*. Like accrued interest and accrued investment income, cash dividends that have been earned but not yet received on stocks that an insurer owns as of the insurer's financial reporting date are reported under *Investment Income Due and Accrued* or a similar asset account. Cash dividends are payable to stockholders who own the stock on the ex-dividend date. The **ex-dividend date**, also called the *ex-date*, is the date used for determining whether a stockholder is eligible to receive a declared cash dividend.

Dividends on common stock are declared by the issuing company's board of directors. Because common stock does not represent a loan, interest is not paid on common stock. Insurers also hold common stock in their separate account portfolios, where they hold the funds used to support variable annuities and other variable products. We discuss separate accounts in Chapter 3. Figure 2-9 presents examples of accounting for cash dividend transactions.

FIGURE 2-9. Cash Dividend Transactions.

The Synchronal Life Insurance Company holds 200 shares of Company A stock in its investment portfolio. Suppose Company A declares a $1 per share cash dividend on its common stock on December 1 for stockholders of record on December 15. Company A will pay the dividend on January 15. In this example, the declaration date is December 1, the ex-dividend date is December 15, and the dividend payment date is January 15.

Accounting Entry on Ex-Dividend Date	**Accounting Entry on Date Dividend is Received**
On December 1, Synchronal would make the following accounting entry to record the cash dividend income due and accrued:	On January 15, upon receiving the cash dividend, Synchronal would record the following accounting entry:

Investment Income
   Due and Accrued 200
     Dividend Income—Common Stock . 200
To record cash dividend income due and accrued.
	Cash 200
	   Investment Income
	       Due and Accrued..........200
	To record a cash dividend received on common stock.

Key Terms and Concepts

securities
short-term assets
long-term assets
tangible assets
intangible assets
debt assets
equity assets
term to maturity
short term
intermediate term
long term
liquidity
cash
cash equivalents
treasury bills
admitted assets
partially admitted assets
nonadmitted assets
valuation
historical cost
book value
current market value
amortized cost
depreciation
amortization
lower of cost or market
   (LCM) rule
net book value
accounting entry
debit
credit
normal balance
on account
account payable
account receivable
invested assets
investing
portfolio

bond
mortgage
stock
stockholder
risk
return
rate of return
risk-return trade-off
corporate bonds
government bonds
bond issuer
bondholder
bond principal
stated rate
interest payment
maturity date
secured bond
collateral
debenture
capital gain
capital loss
realized gain (loss)
unrealized gain (loss)
premium
discount
effective rate of return
collateralized mortgage
   obligations (CMOs)
escrow account
par value of stock
common stock
preferred stock
dividend on stock
cash dividend on stock
stock dividend
moving average market method
ex-dividend date

Chapter 3

Accounting for Other Assets

OBJECTIVES

After reading this chapter, you should be able to

- Recognize the impact of real estate purchases and sales on an insurer's balance sheet

- Demonstrate how insurers can use derivatives to protect an unrealized gain or limit investment risk

- Recognize the impact of policy loans on an insurer's balance sheet

- Describe an insurer's typical short-term assets

- Recognize the purpose of separate accounts

*I*n Chapter 2, we introduced you to an insurer's primary invested assets: bonds, mortgages, and stocks. Chapter 3 continues our discussion of accounting for assets, including real estate, policy loans, cash, and other assets.

Valuation and Reporting of Real Estate

Property is an asset that can be owned or possessed. Property can be classified as real estate or personal property. **Real estate**, also called *real property*, is land or anything attached to the land. Examples of real estate are a parcel of land, a home, or a commercial building. Most insurers own three types of real estate: (1) properties occupied by the insurer, such as home office and regional office buildings, (2) properties held for sale, which are not as common as insurer-occupied properties, and (3) properties held for the production of rental income. **Personal property** is any property that is not real estate. Some examples of personal property are automobiles, computer equipment, and furniture.

Real estate is reported at book value. A property's book value equals the cost of the property, including improvements, less accumulated depreciation, less encumbrances, such as mortgages payable to others that may exist on the property. For U.S. Annual Statement purposes, real estate is typically an admitted asset, but personal property is often classified as a nonadmitted asset. Depreciation on real estate is an investment expense for Annual Statement purposes because an insurer deducts depreciation from gross investment income to determine its net investment income. The insurer describes each item of real estate it owns in a separate schedule of the Annual Statement. For Annual Return purposes, insurers in Canada value real estate using the moving average market method. Both the Annual Statement and the Annual Return contain additional schedules that itemize an insurer's real estate holdings.

Recording Purchases and Sales of Real Estate

Life insurance companies in the United States depreciate the cost of real estate—except for land—over the useful economic life of the property. Besides the purchase price, the cost of real estate may also include any acquisition costs—such as title insurance premiums, sales commissions, and legal fees—spent to acquire the property. Land is never depreciated under U.S. or Canadian accounting standards. Instead, insurers value land at its original cost until selling it.

Recall that, on the date of purchase, the historical cost and the book value of an asset are equal. Over time, however, depreciation will spread or allocate the cost, gain, or loss on the asset. Depreciation for real estate is similar to amortization for stocks and bonds. Insurers in Canada generally do not depreciate any type of real estate. Instead, they record real estate at cost and they use the moving average market method when appropriate. Insurers in Canada can, however, depreciate the cost of improvements to real estate.

Accounting entries to record depreciation on real estate usually involve contra accounts. A **contra account,** which accompanies a specified "companion" account—typically an asset account—is an account that has a normal balance that is the opposite of the companion account. The purpose of a contra account is to provide additional information on the transactions that occur in the companion account. The amounts in a contra account usually decrease the balance in its companion account. However, the monetary amount in a contra account should not be larger than the amount in its companion account. Contra accounts are generally used to amortize real estate depreciation. A typical accounting entry to record depreciation of an insurer's real estate is a debit to *Depreciation on Real Estate* (an expense account) and a credit to a contra account, such as *Accumulated Depreciation on Real Estate.*

By using contra accounts for real estate, an insurer records *Accumulated Depreciation*—a contra account—separately from *Real Estate*—the companion asset account—and thus maintains the original cost of the real estate in its accounting records. Maintaining contra accounts also facilitates preparation of the U.S. Annual Statement and the Canadian Annual Return. Insurers in Canada use *Deferred Realized Gains* instead of *Gain (Loss) on Sale of Real Estate* and amortize the gain (loss) into income, similar to the method used in the sale of stocks. Figure 3-1 presents an example of an insurer's real estate purchase and sale.

Property Taxes

Life insurance companies usually record property taxes as an investment expense. Property taxes are generally payable in advance at specified times during the year. Property taxes accumulate between tax payment dates. Sometimes an insurer purchases real estate for which the taxes have not been paid in advance. In this case, the seller of the real estate either (1) pays to the insurer the amount of any accrued and unpaid taxes or (2) reduces the purchase price by that amount. If an insurer purchases property after the seller has paid the taxes for the current tax period, the insurer must return to the seller the amount of tax applicable to the remainder of the tax

FIGURE 3-1. Real Estate Purchase and Sale.

PURCHASE OF REAL ESTATE

The Mainstay Life Insurance Company, a U.S. life insurance company, purchases Building A for $100,000. The price of the land is not included in the price of the building. Depreciation expense on Building A is $3,000 per year. Mainstay makes the following accounting entry each year to record the building's depreciation:

Depreciation Expense—Building A 3,000
          Accumulated Depreciation—Building A 3,000
To record depreciation expense of $3,000 on Building A.

Accumulated Depreciation—Building A is a contra account. Because a contra account is opposite its companion account, you increase it with a credit entry and decrease it with a debit entry—the *opposite* of increasing and decreasing an asset account. At the end of the first accounting period, Mainstay records the following asset value:

Building A 100,000
          Less Accumulated Depreciation 3,000
Book Value of Building A 97,000

Note that accumulated depreciation does not directly change the monetary value in the *Building A* asset account because depreciation is handled through a contra asset account, called *Accumulated Depreciation—Building A*, instead of the *Building A* asset account. Mainstay reports Building A's book value, which is its cost minus accumulated depreciation. In this example, Building A's book value is $97,000, calculated as $100,000 cost – $3,000 accumulated depreciation. After three years, Mainstay's balance sheet shows Building A with a book value of $91,000 and accumulated depreciation of $9,000, calculated as $100,000 cost – ($3,000 annual depreciation expense × 3 years).

SALE OF REAL ESTATE

Suppose Mainstay sells Building A for $105,000 and that accumulated depreciation to date totals $9,000. The accounting entry to record the sale of this property is as follows:

Cash 105,000
Accumulated Depreciation—Building A 9,000
          Building A 100,000
          Gain on Sale of Building A 14,000
To record the sale of Building A at a gain.

Mainstay calculates the capital gain or capital loss on the sale by subtracting from the sale price Building A's cost, minus any accumulated depreciation. In equation form,

Capital Gain (Loss) = Sale Price – Cost – Accumulated Depreciation
or
Capital Gain (Loss) = Sale Price – Book Value

Thus, in the example above,

Capital Gain (Loss) = 105,000 – (100,000 – 9,000)
= 105,000 – 91,000
= 14,000

Mainstay has a realized capital gain of $14,000, which is credited to *Gain on Sale of Building A*.

Suppose Mainstay sells Building A for $80,000, instead of $105,000. In this case, Mainstay realizes an $11,000 capital loss, calculated as follows: $80,000 sale price – ($100,000 cost – $9,000 accumulated depreciation). The accounting entry to record this transaction is as follows:

Cash 80,000
Accumulated Depreciation on Building A 9,000
Loss on Sale of Real Estate 11,000
          Building A 100,000
To record the sale of Building A at a loss.

period. This concept is similar to that described in the example in Chapter 2, in which both the bond seller and the bond purchaser each earn bond interest income during the same interest period.

Foreclosure

Foreclosure is a legal procedure by which a lender recovers the unpaid loan balance by obtaining title to the real estate offered as collateral if the borrower fails to make timely contractual principal and interest payments on the loan. An insurer has two options when it obtains property through foreclosure: (1) put the property up for resale or (2) rent the property to generate rental income. When real estate obtained through foreclosure is offered for resale, an insurer usually capitalizes the expense for property taxes on the real estate. To *capitalize* an expense means to record the expense as an asset, which, in this case, adds the amount of property taxes to the cost of the property. An insurer treats property taxes as an expense if the insurer obtains property through foreclosure, has completed the foreclosure proceedings, and is renting the property to produce income.

Rental Income and Rental Expense

Earnings associated with real estate ownership generally take the forms of (1) rental income and (2) a gain upon the sale of the property at a price higher than the purchase price. When an insurer leases property to another entity, the insurer records income from this transaction by debiting *Cash* and crediting *Rental Income*. Expense transactions regarding an insurer's rental properties are debited to *Real Estate Expense* and credited to *Cash*. Insurers record the amount of rental income they pay on rented property in an expense account such as *Rental Expense*. We discuss this type of account in Chapter 7.

Derivatives

Insurers typically report derivatives on the balance sheet or disclose them in notes that accompany their financial statements. *Derivatives* are financial assets whose value is based on other securities such as stocks or bonds. For example, stock options are derivatives of stock, an equity security. Most derivatives expire within nine months after they are issued. Types of derivatives that are important to insurers include *options, forward contracts, future contracts,* and *swaps*. **Options** are limited-time contracts that give the owner the right to either buy or sell a specified asset for a stated price. **Forward contracts** and **futures contracts** are limited-time agreements to buy or sell a specified investment in the future for a stated price. **Swaps** are limited-time agreements to exchange the cash flow from one asset for the cash flow from another asset.

Under U.S. GAAP, life insurance companies follow *FASB Statement No. 133: Accounting for Derivative Instruments and Hedging Activities* in determining the values of derivatives. This accounting standard requires each insurer to identify and describe its derivatives and to disclose the risks and the accounting procedures associated with its derivatives. Also, under U.S. GAAP, an insurer typically accounts for its derivatives in the same way that it accounts for the derivatives' underlying securities.

Suppose an insurer purchases derivatives that have a common stock as their underlying security. The insurer would most likely report these derivatives at current market value because this is the valuation method for common stocks. Further, the insurer must recognize and report unrealized gains or losses on these derivatives in the current accounting period, as the insurer cannot defer them. Insight 3-1 presents examples of how an insurer can use specified derivatives to protect an unrealized gain or to exchange a set of cash flows. Further discussion of derivatives is beyond the scope of this textbook.

 Insight 3-1. **Uses for Derivatives.**

Hedging refers to a strategy of investing in a given asset in order to reduce the overall riskiness of a given portfolio's asset mix. For insurers, hedging is often achieved by purchasing various types of options contracts. By holding suitable types of option contracts for their assets, insurers can limit their investment risks arising from unexpected changes in the value of the assets.

One example of a hedging strategy that insurers sometimes use is selling covered call options on their bond investments. A *call option* gives the holder a right to buy bonds at a stated *exercise price* within a limited time. A call option is said to be *covered* if the issuer of the option also owns the optioned bonds. The exercise price is higher than the bonds' market price when the option is written. The seller of the option earns revenue from the sale of the option, even if the option expires unexercised.

If the option holder does exercise the option, the seller is obligated to sell the bonds at the exercise price. The exercise price represents a gain over the bonds' market price at the time the options were written, but less than the bonds' market price when the options are exercised. Thus, if the options are exercised, the option's seller earns a lesser gain on the underlying bonds than the bondholder would have earned if the option had not been sold. By selling a covered call option, an insurance company earns immediate income from the sale of the option, but there are trade-offs: for example, on the insurer's investment in the underlying asset, the insurer gives up the potential for price gains beyond some limit. This limit is related to the option's exercise price, but is not identical to it.

Besides using covered call options to limit investment risks, insurers also use interest-rate swaps. *Interest-rate swaps*, a specific type of swap, are agreements between two parties to exchange a set of cash flows, typically with one based on a fixed interest rate and the other based on a floating interest rate. Interest-rate swaps permit an insurer to in effect convert an existing fixed-rate asset into a "simulated" floating-rate asset, or vice versa. Even though the original asset remains in the insurer's portfolio, the combination of the asset and the swap will have the features of the simulated asset. A discussion of any accounting differences between a true fixed or floating rate bond and a simulated one are beyond the scope of this textbook.

Policy Loans

Many life insurance policies contain a provision giving the policyowner the right to request a policy loan. A **policy loan**, called a *certificate loan* in fraternal benefit societies, is a loan made to a policyowner and secured by a policy's cash surrender value as collateral. A life insurance policy's **cash surrender value**, also called *net cash value,* is the amount of money that the policyowner will receive on a specified date if the policyowner terminates the coverage and surrenders the policy to the insurer. Policy loans differ from an insurer's other invested assets, as shown in Figure 3-2.

The basic accounting entry to record a policy loan is a debit to an asset account such as *Policy Loans* and a credit to *Cash*, another asset account. Accounting for policy loans involves keeping detailed records of the principal and interest on each policy loan. Insurers typically calculate policy loan interest so that it is payable on the policy anniversary date. Some insurers charge policy loan interest at the end of the policy year, and a few insurers charge interest in

FIGURE 3-2. Characteristics of Policy Loans.

➲ The decision to obtain a policy loan comes from the policyowner, not the insurer, because taking out a policy loan is a contractual right of the policyowner.

➲ Policy loans historically were not the best investment for an insurer because interest rates on policy loans were typically lower than what the insurer could obtain through investing in bonds, for example. Most recently issued policies, however, have policy loan interest rates that are tied to market interest rates.

➲ In contrast to other loans, policy loans do not have contractual maturity dates or principal payments, although insurers typically provide policyowners with a predetermined monthly payback schedule that includes policy loan interest.

➲ A policyowner need not pay policy loan interest as long as his or her policy has sufficient cash surrender value plus paid-up additions, if applicable, to secure the loan plus any accrued policy loan interest.

➲ Policy loans do not require systematic repayment plans, as do other loans. An insurer adds unpaid policy loan interest to the amount of the policy loan. If the total of an outstanding loan and its accrued interest exceeds the policy's cash surrender value, however, the policy will terminate without further value, and the insurance contract will no longer be in force. To prevent this from happening, many insurance companies encourage systematic repayment of the principal, and most companies bill annually for policy loan interest.

advance. Policyowners usually pay the accrued policy loan interest when repaying the principal on a policy loan. The typical accounting entry to record the receipt of principal and interest on a policy loan consists of a debit to *Cash*, a credit to *Policy Loans*, and a credit to *Policy Loan Interest*.

On both the U.S. Annual Statement and the Canadian Annual Return, policy loans are reported at book value, which means the original loan amount, plus accrued interest, minus principal repayments. Under both GAAP and statutory accounting practices, insurers report *Policy Loans*, an asset account, separately from *Policy Loan Interest*, a revenue account. However, for financial reporting purposes, policy loan interest that is due and accrued is reported as part of *Investment Income Due and Accrued*, an asset account.

Short-Term Assets

Recall from Chapter 2 that life insurers maintain itemized records for cash, cash equivalents, and other short-term assets available for disbursement of contractual benefits and business expenses. The following sections discuss accounting for cash and cash equivalents and other short-term assets.

Cash and Cash Equivalents

Cash accounting, sometimes called *treasury operations* or *cash management*, refers to the management and maintenance of records for, and the reporting of, all cash transactions, specifically money deposited or withdrawn from an insurer's accounts at a bank or other financial institution. The cash accounting function might also include the investment and management of cash equivalents and short-term invested assets.

Most insurers maintain one or more bank accounts with a bank or other financial institution. For example, an insurer may have separate checking accounts for premium collection, claim payments, and agent commissions. Bank accounts may be interest bearing or non-interest bearing. Interest-bearing bank accounts generally pay a lower rate of interest than is available on short-term investments, such as treasury bills. Therefore, insurers try to keep in bank accounts only the minimum cash balance required to pay their current obligations.

At least monthly, but often more frequently, insurers reconcile the balance in their bank accounts with the bank's balance. Because insurers incur a high volume of transactions through their checking accounts, routine bank reconciliation is especially important. **Bank reconciliation** is the process of identifying and explaining the difference between (1) the balance presented on the bank statement and (2) the balance in the insurer's accounting records, sometimes referred to as the *book balance*.

An insurer's checking account book balance rarely matches the bank balance because of timing differences, adjustments, and errors, some of which are listed in Figure 3-3. Most timing differences are a result of specific transactions that have cleared either the insurer's records or the bank's records, but not both. A detailed discussion of bank reconciliation procedures is beyond the scope of this textbook.

For financial reporting purposes, an insurer's cash balance as of a specified date is the total amount of cash in its *Cash* account. Under both GAAP and statutory accounting practices, the insurer reports

FIGURE 3-3. Timing Differences, Adjustments, and Errors.

Outstanding checks are checks that the insurer has written, deducted from its book balance, and sent to payees, but which have not yet cleared the bank. As a result, the bank has not yet deducted them from the bank balance.	**Unrecorded deposits,** also called *deposits in transit*, are those deposits that the insurer added to its book balance after the closing date on the bank statement. Therefore, the bank has not yet added them to the bank balance.	**Service charges** include charges for account service, check processing, and stop payment orders. Usually, the insurer learns the amount of its service charges when it reviews its bank statement.
An insurer earns **interest income** if the checking account is interest bearing. The amount of interest income earned will appear on the bank statement. The bank has already added this amount to the bank balance, but the insurer may not know the exact amount of the interest income until the bank statement arrives.	**Nonsufficient funds (NSF) checks** are checks that have "bounced"; in other words, the payor did not have enough money in his or her checking account to pay the amount of the check. Although insurance companies rarely write NSF checks, they sometimes receive NSF checks from customers. When an insurer receives a check, the insurer assumes that the check is good, adds the amount of the check to its book balance, and sends the check as a deposit to its bank. The insurer must deduct the amount of any NSF checks from its book balance to reconcile its bank statement.	**Errors** made by the bank or the insurer may result in a discrepancy in the checking account balance. Typically, an insurer finds errors by investigating the reasons for differences between the bank balance and the insurer's book balance. Often this involves tracing each transaction from the date that the checking account last balanced with the bank through the closing date indicated on the latest bank statement. If the bank made the error, the insurer notifies the bank, which in turn corrects its records. If the insurer made the error, then the insurer makes the appropriate accounting entries to correct the error.

this amount on the U.S. Annual Statement or Canadian Annual Return and the annual report, if applicable. Besides cash and cash equivalents, insurers also have other short-term assets. Short-term assets, with the exception of prepaid expenses, are typically reported as admitted assets on the U.S. Annual Statement. The following sections describe accounting and financial reporting for (1) investment income due and accrued, (2) deferred premiums and uncollected premiums, and (3) prepaid expenses.

Investment Income Due and Accrued

Investment income due and accrued is a short-term asset for insurers in the United States. **Due income** is income that was expected by the insurer before the financial reporting date but that has not yet been received. A rent payment due on December 15, but which the insurer has not received by December 31, is an example of due income. Due income is earned and should have been received, but was not received, during the same accounting period.

Accrued income consists of income that the insurer has already earned, but which is not receivable until a specified date in the next accounting period—that is, income that is due *after* the insurer's financial reporting date. Accrued income is thus earned during one accounting period, but not receivable until a later accounting period. For example, an insurer reports bond interest earned in December but not receivable until the following January as accrued investment income on the income statement. Both due income and accrued income are classified as assets because the insurer can legally expect to receive the income as a result of a contractual arrangement. *Investment Income Due and Accrued* is the account used to report due income and accrued income on the U.S. Annual Statement. *Accrued Investment Income* is the equivalent account on the Canadian Annual Return.

Deferred Premiums and Uncollected Premiums

In setting policy premium rates for life insurance, insurers generally assume that all premiums are paid on an annual basis at the beginning of the policy year. Most customers pay their life insurance premiums in cash or by check on or before the policy issue date or policy anniversary date. However, policy premiums may be paid in installments more frequently than annually, such as on a monthly or quarterly basis. Life insurers therefore employ short-term asset accounts—such as *Deferred Premiums* or *Uncollected Premiums*—to record and report policy premiums that were due, but which have not been received by the insurer.

Deferred premiums are life insurance premiums due after the date of the U.S. Annual Statement but before the next policy anniversary date and the next Annual Statement date. Suppose a life insurance policy has a policy anniversary date of August 15 and an annual premium of $1,000, due on July 1. In this example, the policy premium is due after December 31 of the current year, but before August 15—the policy anniversary date—and before December 31—the next Annual Statement date. Thus, this premium is classified as a deferred premium. The *Deferred Premiums* account is specific to life insurance companies in the United States. This account applies only to life insurance premium payments that (1) are made more frequently than annually and that (2) have a due date that falls between the U.S. Annual Statement date and the policy's next anniversary date.

Establishing an asset account for deferred premiums is exclusive to the U.S. Annual Statement, because insurers in Canada use different methods to calculate contractual reserves. We discuss contractual reserves in Chapter 4. Life insurance companies report their uncollected premiums on the U.S. Annual Statement or the Canadian Annual Return. *Uncollected premiums*, called *premiums outstanding* on the Canadian Annual Return, are life insurance policy premiums that are due before the financial reporting date, but the insurer has not received these premiums as of that date.

Prepaid Expenses

In accounting, *prepaid expenses* are those expenditures, remitted in advance, that the insurer expects will provide a future value or benefit. Examples of prepaid expenses include rents, subscriptions, service contracts, and any other fees or charges that the insurer has paid before receiving the goods and services associated with those charges. Under statutory accounting, prepaid expenses are nonadmitted assets because prepaid expenses often lack liquidity. In other words, the insurer may have difficulty converting prepaid expenses into cash quickly for an approximation of their true value. Under GAAP, however, prepaid expenses are classified as short-term assets and charged to the accounting period in which the benefits of the prepaid products or services are received or used. Further, prepaid expenses typically provide a company with benefits in the short term.

Deferred Acquisition Costs

Deferred acquisition costs (DAC), also called *deferred policy acquisition costs (DPAC)*, are costs reported under U.S. GAAP that are related primarily and directly to acquiring new business and retaining current business associated with new insurance products.

Under U.S. GAAP, insurers in the United States capitalize these costs and then amortize them over the premium-paying periods of the products. Costs that may be deferred in this manner include policy issue costs, product development costs, and agent commissions. *Deferred Acquisition Costs* is a long-term asset account that appears on a balance sheet prepared under U.S. GAAP, but not on the U.S. Annual Statement. Insurers in Canada include acquisition costs in their reserve calculations, so there is no need to establish an asset account to defer these costs under Canadian GAAP.

Separate Accounts

Insurers purchase assets for their general account and one or more separate accounts:

- For insurers, the **general account** is the portfolio of assets backing an insurer's guaranteed products, such as whole life insurance and fixed-rate annuities.

- For insurers, a **separate account**, called a *segregated fund* or a *segregated account* in Canada, is a separate portfolio that is used to support nonguaranteed insurance products—such as variable life insurance and variable annuities—in which the customer shares or assumes investment risk.

Figure 3-4 summarizes the differences between an insurer's general account and its separate accounts.

Insurers in the United States itemize their separate account assets and liabilities on the Separate Accounts Annual Statement, where these items are generally reported at current market value. Life insurers in the United States are not required to prepare a Separate Accounts Annual Statement if the insurer offers only guaranteed insurance products. However, life insurers that offer only variable products or a combination of guaranteed and nonguaranteed insurance products must prepare both the Separate Accounts Annual Statement and the Annual Statement.

Typically, transactions associated with premium income for both guaranteed and nonguaranteed products are reported on the Annual Statement, whereas transactions associated with the investment of premium income for nonguaranteed insurance products are reported on the Separate Account Annual Statement. For example, an insurer reports premium income received on its variable life insurance products on the Annual Statement, but reports how this money was invested on the Separate Account Annual Statement. Insurers in Canada report their segregated funds at current market value on the Segregated Funds Annual Return.

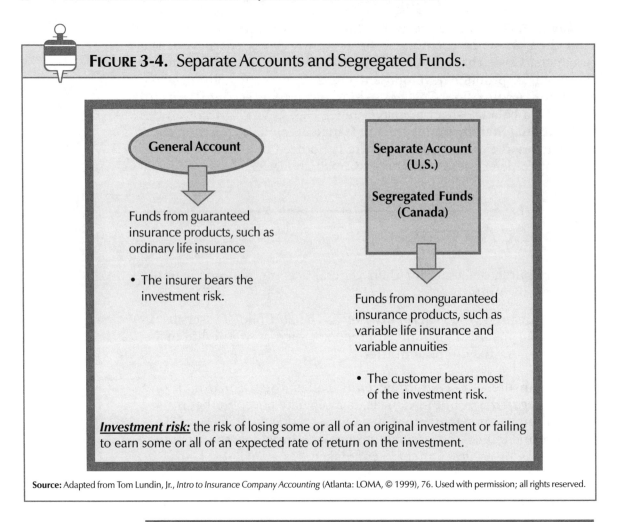

FIGURE 3-4. Separate Accounts and Segregated Funds.

General Account

Funds from guaranteed insurance products, such as ordinary life insurance

• The insurer bears the investment risk.

Separate Account (U.S.)

Segregated Funds (Canada)

Funds from nonguaranteed insurance products, such as variable life insurance and variable annuities

• The customer bears most of the investment risk.

**Investment risk:** the risk of losing some or all of an original investment or failing to earn some or all of an expected rate of return on the investment.

Source: Adapted from Tom Lundin, Jr., _Intro to Insurance Company Accounting_ (Atlanta: LOMA, © 1999), 76. Used with permission; all rights reserved.

Key Terms and Concepts

property
real estate
personal property
contra account
foreclosure
capitalize
derivatives
options
forward contracts
future contracts
swaps
hedging
interest-rate swaps
policy loan
cash surrender value
cash accounting

bank reconciliation
outstanding checks
unrecorded deposits
nonsufficient funds (NSF)
    checks
due income
accrued income
deferred premiums
uncollected premiums
prepaid expenses
deferred acquisition costs
    (DAC)
general account
separate account
investment risk

Chapter 4

Accounting for Reserves

OBJECTIVES

After reading this chapter, you should be able to

🌐 Recognize the purpose of reserves in the insurance industry

🌐 Distinguish among contractual reserves, noncontractual reserves, modified reserves, net reserves, and gross reserves

🌐 Demonstrate the prospective method and the retrospective method of calculating contractual reserves

🌐 Recognize features of the policy premium method used for setting reserve amounts in Canada

🌐 Demonstrate an understanding of surplus strain and how it can be relieved by modified reserve methods

*I*n this chapter, we discuss the effect that different accounting systems have on an insurer's reserve accounts and the assumptions that actuaries use to calculate reserve liabilities. Then, we examine several types of reserves, including the contractual reserves that insurers maintain to support their obligations under life insurance policies.

The Concept of Reserves

In the context of accounting for life insurance transactions, *reserves* are estimates of the amounts of money that an insurer needs to pay future business obligations. Reserves make up most of an insurer's liabilities. Because an insurer's reserves represent significant amounts of money, they are a key factor in the insurer's financial position. Thus, insurance companies and regulators place great emphasis on establishing adequate reserves. For some insurance products, determining the amount of a reserve is a relatively straightforward process. However, for most insurance products, the amount of an insurer's future business obligations is not known precisely in advance. Therefore, insurers must set reasonable reserve amounts by identifying and consistently applying the proper (1) values for actuarial assumptions, (2) reserve valuation methods, and (3) procedures for ensuring reasonable values for reserves.

Actuarial Assumptions and Reserves

The amounts that insurers record in their reserve accounts are, of necessity, estimates. When an insurer establishes reserves for a block of guaranteed insurance policies, it knows the total face value of the block of policies, and, thus, its future obligation to its customers. However, the insurer can only estimate the amount of investment earnings on the policy premiums it invests. Further, the insurer does not know precisely *when* a customer or beneficiary will submit a claim on the policy or *if* a policy will lapse before benefit payments become due.

Because of such uncertainties, insurers must estimate the amounts to report in their reserve accounts. Each assumed value used in life insurance product design is known as an *actuarial assumption*. To determine the amount of reserves to record in its accounting records, insurers rely on actuaries. An *actuary* is an expert in the mathematics of insurance, annuities, and financial instruments. In insurance companies, actuaries are responsible for ensuring that the products are financially sound. Using mathematical probabilities, actuaries estimate the amounts needed to pay future benefits to the insurer's customers. The insurer then records and reports these amounts as liabilities in its accounting records. Actuaries usually estimate reserves on the basis of a block of policies, instead of each individual policy. Reserves for a block of policies are called *aggregate reserves*.

Reserves and the Basic Accounting Equation

On a mutual insurance company's balance sheet, surplus (an owners' equity account) is found by subtracting liabilities from assets, as shown:

$$\text{Assets} - \text{Liabilities} = \text{Surplus}$$

Let's consider how each of these terms relates to a life insurance product. We can view a given product's assets on a specified date as being an approximation of the product's collected premiums plus accumulated interest earnings. The product liability consists of the reserve for that product. Thus, the product's surplus is the difference between the product's assets and its reserves. The product's surplus is the amount that the product contributes to the insurer's overall capital and surplus (owners' equity), and thus to the insurer's solvency and profitability.

Types of Accounting Records

Insurers must keep different sets of accounting records for different purposes. For insurers operating in the United States, these various sets of accounting records are based on statutory accounting practices, generally accepted accounting principles (GAAP), internal (modified GAAP) accounting practices, and tax accounting practices. These sets of accounting records give rise to reserves that are respectively labeled (1) statutory reserves, also known as required reserves and solvency-basis reserves; (2) GAAP reserves, also known as profitability-basis reserves; (3) internal reserves; and (4) tax reserves. Insurers operating in Canada maintain Canadian GAAP reserves and tax reserves. Each set of accounting records meets a distinct need for financial reporting, as follows:

- **Statutory accounting records**, also called *solvency-basis accounting records*, are designed for financial reporting to state insurance regulators, whose primary interest is in evaluating insurance companies' solvency and long-term financial stability. For Canada, separate statutory accounting records do not exist. However, insurers in a number of other countries use solvency-basis accounting for some purposes.

- **GAAP accounting records** are designed for financial reporting to investors and the public at large. These records focus on showing the company's financial stability along with its profitability. Thus, GAAP is a type of profitability-basis accounting. U.S. GAAP differs considerably from Canadian GAAP. Insurers in Canada use Canadian GAAP accounting records for reporting to insurance regulators.

- **Internal accounting records**, also known as *modified GAAP accounting records*, are designed for financial reporting to company management, whose main interest is in having appropriate data for making decisions. Internal accounting systems are designed to produce results that management believes present a realistic picture of a company's financial situation. For internal accounting, each insurer freely sets its own desired accounting standards. Further discussion of internal accounting systems is included in LOMA's *The Accounting Function and Management Accounting in Life Insurance Companies*.

- **Tax accounting records** are designed for financial reporting to taxation authorities in the United States and Canada. Tax issues, including tax reserves, are outside of the scope of our discussion.

For much of our discussion, differences among the accounting systems will be irrelevant. However, when appropriate, we discuss specific requirements affecting specific sets of reserves. Figure 4-1 summarizes our discussion of accounting records and reserves.

Contractual Reserves and Noncontractual Reserves

Insurers have several types of contractual reserves and noncontractual reserves for life insurance. **Contractual reserves** are accounting liabilities that identify the amount that, together with future premiums and interest earnings, represents the expected amount of future benefits payable on an insurer's in-force business—that is, the insurer's obligations to its customers—as follows:

$$\text{Reserve} + \text{Future premiums} + \text{Interest earnings} = \text{Expected future benefits payable on in-force business}$$

FIGURE 4-1. U.S. and Canadian Insurance Accounting Records and their Audiences.

Accounting Records	Primary Audience	Reserve Used
U.S. statutory	Insurance regulators	U.S. statutory reserves
U.S. GAAP	Potential investors	U.S. GAAP reserves
Canadian GAAP	Insurance regulators and potential investors	Canadian GAAP reserves
Internal	Company managers	Internal reserves
Tax basis	Taxing authorities	Tax reserves

Other terms sometimes used for contractual reserves include *policy reserves*, *legal reserves*, *tabular reserves*, and *statutory reserves* in the United States and *required reserves*, *provision for future policy benefits*, and *net actuarial liabilities* in Canada. Insurers in the United States must calculate contractual reserves according to criteria specified under state standard valuation laws for guaranteed and nonguaranteed products. **Noncontractual reserves** represent insurers' business obligations that are not directly attributable to paying benefits for a specified product. All types of reserves that are not contractual are classified as noncontractual reserves.

Claim Reserves

Insurers also establish claim reserves for pending financial obligations to customers. **Claim reserves**, which typically consist of *disabled life reserves* and *active life reserves*, are liability accounts that identify the future amounts that an insurer will pay on claims that have been reported to the insurer before the date of the financial statement but have not yet been paid in full as of that date. In other words, the insurer is aware of its obligation to settle specified claims, but has not yet done so. Claim reserves are primarily associated with policies that have ongoing losses such as accident and health insurance policies, rather than a single loss, as is the case with most life insurance policies. However, insurers establish claim reserves for pending life insurance claims, which are claims that have been received but have not yet been processed for payment. Insurers establish claim reserves for a variety of pending claim payments, as shown in Figure 4-2.

FIGURE 4-2. Categories of Pending Claims.

Pending Claims	Incurred?	Reported?	Approved?	Paid?
Incurred but not yet reported (IBNR)	Yes	No	No	No
Reported but not yet approved	Yes	Yes	No	No
Approved but not yet paid	Yes	Yes	Yes	No
Approved but not yet paid in full	Yes	Yes	Yes	Ongoing
Reported but denied	Yes	Yes	No	No

Reserve Valuation Methods

Insurers use several approaches for calculating contractual reserves. A *reserve valuation method* is an approach for calculating reserve amounts. The insurer's final realized profit or loss on a product will not be affected by a reserve valuation method. However, the reserve valuation method can strongly affect the timing of a product's reported earnings.

Gross and Net Reserve Valuation Methods

Reserves can be calculated on a gross basis or a net basis. A **gross reserve valuation method** is a method of computing reserves that makes explicit provision for the insurer's product-related expenses or loading. Gross reserve valuation methods are not used in the United States for financial reporting. Reserves developed using a gross reserve valuation method are sometimes known as **gross reserves**. For their solvency-basis reserves used for reporting to regulators, a few countries require the use of some form of gross reserve valuation method. These countries include Australia, Canada, and France.[1]

Most reserve valuation methods used in the United States are net reserve valuation methods. A **net reserve valuation method** is a method of computing reserves that does not make explicit provision for the insurer's product-related expenses or loading. Reserves developed using a net reserve valuation method are sometimes known as **net reserves**. For solvency-basis reserves, many regulatory authorities require the use of some form of net reserve valuation method. Net reserve valuation methods are required in Argentina, Brazil, Chile, Germany, Italy, Japan, Malaysia, Mexico, The Netherlands, Singapore, South Africa, Spain, Taiwan, the United Kingdom, and the United States.[2]

Modified Reserve Valuation Methods

A **modified reserve valuation method**, a way of calculating U.S. statutory reserves, permits an insurer to set a lower-than-level first-year contractual reserve in recognition of the surplus strain from a product's first-year expenses. Under a modified reserve method, the first-year reserve adjustment then affects the statutory reserve values for all subsequent years. A reserve developed using a modified reserve valuation method is known as a **modified reserve**. For U.S. statutory reserve valuation, insurers can relieve surplus strain by using modified reserve valuation methods. We discuss surplus strain later in this chapter.

Prospective and Retrospective Reserve Valuation Methods

Insurers in the United States use two approaches to net reserve valuation methods: (1) the prospective method and (2) the retrospective method. As used in the United States, both methods always yield the same reserve amount when applied to the same valuation problem and when using the same actuarial assumptions as to interest, mortality, and lapses. In some cases, one method or the other is better suited to a specific product type.

Statutory requirements in the United States specify the minimum size of insurers' contractual reserves, but do not specify a maximum size. Further, U.S. GAAP contractual reserves, Canadian GAAP contractual reserves, and several other types of reserves form the basis for the insurer's projections of future conditions. Insurers have considerable discretion concerning the valuation method used to calculate these reserves. Figure 4-3 summarizes common valuation methods for calculating contractual reserves.

FIGURE 4-3. Reserve Valuation Methods.

PROSPECTIVE RESERVE VALUATION METHOD

A *prospective reserve valuation method* for estimating a value for a contractual reserve liability involves finding the present value of a contract's future cash flows—its future premiums and future benefit payments. Under the prospective method, the net reserve for a block of contracts is calculated according to the following equation:

$$\text{Prospective contractual reserve} = \text{Present value of future benefits} - \text{Present value of future net premiums}$$

The *present value of future benefits* equals the net single premium at the insured's attained age for the remaining policy benefits. The *net single premium* is the actuarial present value at issue of a product's future benefit costs. For life insurance, the *present value of future net premiums* is the present value of a life annuity due. The concept of present value is outside the scope of our discussion.

RETROSPECTIVE RESERVE VALUATION METHOD (U.S.)

A *retrospective reserve valuation method* for setting a contractual reserve liability involves finding the accumulated values of a contract's past cash flows—its past premiums and past benefit payments. For a given product, the *accumulated value of net premiums* at any time is equal to the total of net premiums collected, accumulated at interest. For a given product, the *accumulated cost of insurance* at any time is the total of benefits paid, accumulated at interest. Under the retrospective method, the net reserve for a block of contracts is calculated according to the following equation:

$$\text{Retrospective contractual reserve} = \text{Accumulated value of net premiums} - \text{Accumulated cost of insurance}$$

POLICY PREMIUM METHOD (CANADA)

Insurers in Canada must use the policy premium method of reserve valuation. The *policy premium method (PPM)* is a type of prospective gross reserve valuation method. The PPM contractual reserve is equal to the difference between the present value of future benefits and the present value of future gross premiums. The PPM formula includes a provision for loading. Thus, the value of future benefits under the PPM formula includes estimated future maintenance expenses and future excess interest credits. Insurers in Canada calculate contractual reserves using the following equation:

$$\text{PPM contractual reserve} = \text{Present value of future benefits} - \text{Present value of future } \textit{gross} \text{ premiums}$$

Life Insurance Reserves

At any time, the retrospective contractual reserve for a block of life insurance policies represents the excess of the premiums over benefits, plus the interest earned up to that time, as shown:

Life insurance contractual reserve	=	Net premiums received	−	Benefits paid earnings	+	Interest earnings

At most times, the insurer has received more money in net premiums than it has paid out in benefits on a block of life insurance business. The insurer invests the excess of net premiums over benefits. The insurer uses this excess, plus the interest earned from investing it, plus any future net premiums, to pay the benefits that become due later in the life of the block of policies, as shown:

Life insurance contractual reserve	+	Future net premiums	+	Future interest earnings	=	Total future benefits

Because the insurer must hold an amount of assets that at least equals the contractual reserve, the reserve helps ensure that the insurer will have the assets it needs to pay benefits.

Reserve Strengthening or Destrengthening

An insurer sometimes decides that the reserves for an existing product or block of policies are too low, and might then decide to increase the reserves. In such a situation, the insurer can engage in *reserve strengthening*—increasing the amount of its reserves. An insurer may strengthen its reserves if its experience with a product reveals that the assumptions used to calculate contractual reserves were too optimistic. In such a situation, the insurer may decide to strengthen its reserves to protect its rating or its solvency. To do so, however, decreases capital and surplus, thus leaving fewer funds available for future growth.

Insurers can strengthen reserves by using actuarial assumptions that are less favorable to the company than those used in the original reserve valuation. On the other hand, if reserves are too conservative, an insurer may engage in *reserve destrengthening*—decreasing the amount of its reserves. When an insurer decreases its liabilities by destrengthening its reserves, the insurer increases its capital and surplus. The insurer can then use the increased capital for other purposes, such as to support new business. In the United States, reserve destrengthening requires regulatory permission from the insurance commissioner in its state of domicile, whereas in Canada no permission is needed to destrengthen reserves. However, in practice, insurers rarely destrengthen their contractual reserves. Note that the periodic accounting entries made to increase or decrease aggregate contractual reserves as a result of routine contractual activity differs from reserve strengthening or reserve destrengthening. In the case of accounting entries to report routine contractual activity, only the dollar amount of the reserve changes, not the insurer's underlying actuarial assumptions.

Regulatory requirements determine the minimum size of an insurer's statutory reserves at the time a product is issued. Thereafter, if the insurer's statutory reserves are equal to the legal minimum, the insurer cannot destrengthen its reserves. However, if an insurer's reserves are larger than the law requires, then the insurer may be able to destrengthen its statutory reserves, as long as the reserves remain at least as large as those required by law. The accounting treatment for reserve strengthening and destrengthening involves a direct change to an insurer's balance sheet, whereas a routine change in reserves goes through the income statement.

Under U.S. GAAP, as opposed to statutory requirements, insurers normally *cannot* alter their actuarial assumptions to change the strength of their reserves. Throughout the life of the policy, an insurer must calculate GAAP reserves using the insurer's assumptions at the time of policy issue. In Canada, unlike in the United States, insurers can change their actuarial assumptions every year to reflect their emerging experience and their new expectations for the future. Thus, insurers in Canada can strengthen or destrengthen reserves as needed without obtaining regulatory permission. The Canadian Institute of Actuaries (CIA) provides guidelines to help insurers select the sets of actuarial assumptions used in scenario analysis for reserve valuations. Insurers operating in Canada, however, must submit a qualified valuation actuary's formal certification that a reserve valuation conforms to professional standards of actuarial practice set by the CIA.

Statutory and GAAP Reserves

For insurers in the United States, the calculation of GAAP contractual reserves differs in several ways from that of statutory reserves. An insurer calculates GAAP reserves for fixed-premium products based on its expectations at policy issue for mortality, interest, and withdrawals. The expectations determined at policy issue typically apply for the life of the policy. U.S. GAAP generally does not allow insurers to modify the basis on which they calculate reserves, even if the insurer's expectations at policy issue turn out to be wrong. In contrast, under certain conditions, insurers can strengthen or destrengthen their statutory contractual reserves after business has been in force by altering the assumptions used to calculate the reserves.

Another important difference between the calculation of GAAP and statutory reserves is the nature of the present value of future benefits under each system. For statutory reserves, the present value of future benefits includes only one element—the present value of future death benefits—because the statutory assumption is that all policies remain in force. Under GAAP, the present value of future benefits includes the:

- Present value of future death benefits

- Present value of future benefits from surrendered or lapsed policies

- Present value of all expected policy dividends

- Present value of the insurer's expected maintenance expenses for the business

Under U.S. GAAP, reserve calculations for fixed-premium products are based primarily on the insurer's expected results for mortality, investment return, and withdrawals. In contrast, statutory reserves are based on prescribed mortality rates, contractual interest rates, and a lapse rate of zero. Three models for reserves exist for U.S. GAAP reserves. The model we focus on in this section is the *provision for adverse deviation*, which is contained in *FASB Statement No. 60*. By definition, the **provision for adverse deviation** is a safety margin to allow for unfavorable variations from actuarial assumptions. Adding this safety margin increases the size of GAAP reserves for U.S. stock insurers. Nevertheless, GAAP reserves generally are considerably smaller than statutory reserves. Figure 4-4 summarizes the characteristics of statutory and GAAP contractual reserves in the United States.

Figure 4-5 presents a review of types of reserves. The definitions of reserves in Figure 4-5 are not mutually exclusive. For example, a specified reserve could properly be described as a contractual reserve, modified reserve, U.S. statutory reserve, and net reserve.

FIGURE 4-4. U.S. GAAP Reserves and Statutory Reserves.

U.S. GAAP Reserves

- Calculated using basic mortality tables, which contain realistic mortality rates, although they may also include a provision for adverse deviation

- Calculated using a realistic interest rate

- Calculated assuming a realistic withdrawal rate

- Future benefits include death benefits and, where appropriate, surrender benefits, dividends, and maintenance expenses

Statutory Reserves

- Calculated using valuation mortality tables, which contain a safety margin

- Calculated using a lower-than-anticipated interest rate

- Calculated assuming no withdrawals

- Future benefits include death benefits only

Accounting for Reserve Liabilities

Whenever you see reserves on an insurer's balance sheet, you are looking at an aggregate number for each line of business. Typically, changes in contractual reserves are reported at the end of an accounting period for that period's transactions. Typical accounts used to record such changes include *Change in Reserves* or *Increases/Decreases in Provision for Future Policy Benefits*, which are income statement accounts, and *Contractual Reserves—Life* or *Claim Reserves—Life*, which are balance sheet accounts. The insurer also reports reserves for each type of insurance product in the U.S. Annual Statement or Canadian Annual Return. Figure 4-6 presents an example of how insurers typically account for their reserve liabilities.

FIGURE 4-5. Reserve Types.

U.S. statutory reserve	◆	A reserve established and reported according to the reporting requirements applicable to insurers operating in the United States
U.S. GAAP reserve	◆	A reserve established and reported according to generally accepted accounting principles (GAAP) established by the Financial Accounting Standards Board (FASB) for insurers operating in the United States
Canadian GAAP reserve	◆	A reserve established and reported according to generally accepted accounting principles (GAAP) established for insurers operating in Canada
Internal reserve	◆	A reserve—also known as a modified GAAP reserve—established for an insurer's internal accounting purposes, and intended for use in management decisions, but not for financial reporting purposes
Tax reserve	◆	A reserve established according to the requirements for tax reporting
Contractual reserve	◆	A liability that identifies the amount that, together with future premiums and interest earnings, represents the expected amount of future benefits payable on an insurer's in-force business
Noncontractual reserve	◆	A reserve that is not directly attributable to paying benefits on a specified insurance product
Gross reserve	◆	A reserve that includes in its calculation an insurer's expenses of issuing and supporting a contract
Net reserve	◆	A reserve that does not include in its calculation an insurer's expenses of issuing and supporting a contract
Prospective reserve	◆	A reserve that is calculated by finding the present values of a contract's future cash flows—its future premiums and future benefit payments
Retrospective reserve	◆	A reserve that is calculated by finding the accumulated values of a contract's past cash flows—its past premiums and past benefit payments
Net GAAP reserve	◆	An insurer's reported U.S. GAAP reserves minus deferred acquisition costs (DAC)
Modified reserve	◆	A reserve developed using a modified reserve valuation method

Part of the aggregate reserve amount is *released* when a policy benefit is paid or a contract terminates. A ***released reserve*** is a contractual reserve that was originally established in connection with an in-force policy but is no longer required. Again, changes in

FIGURE 4-6. Accounting for Reserve Liabilities.

The first-quarter balance sheet of the Mindful Life Insurance Company reports $2.5 million in contractual reserves for life insurance policies. During the second quarter, Mindful has a higher volume of benefit payments and higher benefit amounts for each claim than the actuaries originally projected. For this example, assume that no new policies were sold in this block of business during the first and second quarters. Actuaries review Mindful's second-quarter transactions for benefit payments to recalculate the amount of contractual reserves. The actuaries have determined that $2.7 million is a better estimate of Mindful's contractual reserves, given this additional information. Mindful then records the following accounting entry to update its contractual reserves for financial reporting purposes:

Change in Reserves—Life 200,000
     Contractual Reserves—Life 200,000

To adjust upward the amount of contractual reserves on the balance sheet.

Mindful reports $2.7 million in contractual reserves on its balance sheet for the second quarter. Had the updated reserve amount been $2.4 million instead of $2.7 million, the accounting entry would have decreased reserves by $100,000 ($2.5 million – $2.4 million), as follows:

Contractual Reserves—Life 100,000
     Change in Reserves—Life...100,000

To adjust downward the amount of contractual reserves on the balance sheet.

reserves typically are recorded at the end of each accounting period. Therefore, it may be difficult to see during an accounting period the interrelationship among reserves, premium income, and changes in other account classifications such as assets and surplus. Figure 4-7 presents a simplified flowchart of the accounting entries resulting from financial transactions associated with a block of insurance contracts.

Surplus Strain

So far in this chapter, when illustrating the prospective and retrospective methods of calculating contractual reserves as practiced in the United States, we have used the net level premium approach to calculate contractual reserves. The **net level premium approach**

FIGURE 4-7. Flowchart of the Effect of Reserves on Other Accounts.

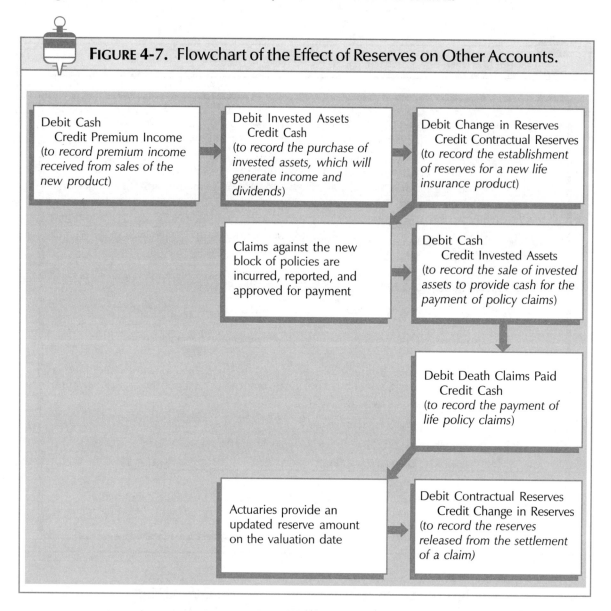

assumes that the amount of a policy's net premiums does not increase or decrease during the life of the policy. Recall that insurers in the United States typically use one of two variations of this approach: (1) the *prospective reserve valuation method* and (2) the *retrospective reserve valuation method*.

However, using the net level premium approach to calculate contractual reserves for such products as ordinary life insurance can create a condition called *surplus strain*. **Surplus strain**, also known as *issue strain* or *new business strain*, is the decrease in an insurer's surplus caused by the high first-year costs and the reserving requirements associated with new products. Any arrangement to diminish potential surplus strain is referred to as **surplus relief**. Surplus strain is especially important under statutory accounting because all costs are expensed in the current accounting period. Recall from Chapter 3 that, under U.S. GAAP, specified first-year costs are classified as an asset known as deferred acquisition costs, which are capitalized in the current accounting period and expensed in future accounting periods.

An insurer's first-year costs for many products are substantial. In addition, the insurer must establish reserves for a product in the product's first year. The increase in a U.S. insurer's assets resulting from a product's first-year premium is often smaller than the increase in the insurer's liabilities created by the reserve the insurer must establish for the product. In such situations, the insurer's surplus must be reduced to provide for the increase in reserves.

For a new product, first-year costs of contract issue, sales commissions, and the creation of new reserves typically combine to produce a negative first-year surplus. This negative surplus is an aspect of surplus strain. Under U.S. statutory and U.S. GAAP accounting, insurers use different approaches for spreading out the impact of surplus strain. In brief, U.S. statutory accounting provides for specially adjusted reserves known as *modified reserves*, but makes no special provision for adjusting assets. U.S. GAAP spreads out the impact of first-year expenses on surplus by means of an asset account known as deferred acquisition costs (DAC), and provides for no adjustment to reserve liabilities. Figure 4-8 summarizes adjustments for surplus strain under U.S. GAAP and statutory reporting. The following sections discuss the use of deferred acquisition costs and reinsurance to reduce surplus strain.

Deferred Acquisition Costs (U.S. GAAP)

U.S. GAAP reduces surplus strain by permitting insurers to spread out, in a process known as *amortization*, the reporting of acquisition costs and issue costs over several years. In order to keep their

FIGURE 4-8. Reducing Surplus Strain for U.S. Reporting Purposes.

	U.S. reporting basis	
	GAAP	**Statutory**
Adjustment mechanism	Deferred acquisition costs (DAC)	Modified reserves
Balance sheet item adjusted	GAAP assets	Statutory reserves

GAAP accounts balanced when reserves are amortized, insurers must create an asset account called *Deferred Acquisition Costs (DAC)*. Recall from Chapter 3 that *Deferred Acquisition Costs* is the asset account insurers establish to spread out the reporting of first-year costs such as acquisition costs and policy issue costs. Then, the negative impact on surplus is applied in subsequent years. Note that DAC is not a tool for increasing or decreasing the amount of a reserve. Because of the presence of DAC, when analysts use U.S. GAAP financial statements to evaluate an insurer's strength, they typically adjust GAAP reserves for DAC to produce a measure known as net GAAP reserves. *Net GAAP reserves* equal the insurer's reported GAAP reserves minus DAC, as shown:

$$\text{Net GAAP reserves} = \text{GAAP reserves} - \text{DAC}$$

Net GAAP reserves are similar to modified statutory reserves in that both net GAAP reserves and modified statutory reserves represent the insurer's contractual reserve liabilities modified by an allowance to reflect the high cost of first-year expenses. Remember, reserves and surplus are both on the right-hand side of the basic accounting equation. If assets cannot be increased to match the increase in reserves, then surplus must be decreased to create the balance. Because of the use of the policy premium method (PPM) to establish reserves, surplus strain is generally less severe in Canada than in the United States. According to the PPM, the contractual reserve calculated using gross premiums is smaller than the contractual reserve calculated using net premiums. With this smaller reserve, surplus strain is thus less severe.

Reinsurance and Reserve Credits

Reinsurance is a transaction between two insurance companies in which one company—called the *reinsurer* or the *assuming company*—agrees to take on (assume) some of the insurance risks of another insurance company—called the *ceding company*. The reinsurer agrees to pay claims on a portion of the ceding company's insurance business. A ceding company uses reinsurance primarily to reduce the amount of risk it assumes when it sells an insurance policy. An insurer also considers its retention limit and the conditions of the reinsurance agreement in calculating reserves for reinsured insurance policies. For a specified group of insureds or contracts, the maximum amount of coverage per life that an insurer will keep at its own risk, without ceding a portion of the risk to a reinsurer, is called the insurer's *retention limit*. The retention limit can be different for each type of insurance a company sells.

Under some types of indemnity reinsurance arrangements, the reinsurer assumes some of the insurer's liability for benefit payments and also agrees to establish reserves for the reinsured portion of the risk. Under these agreements, an insurer is responsible for establishing a smaller amount of required reserves, and has a reduced potential for surplus strain. The reduction in surplus strain that is achieved by using reinsurance is a type of surplus relief. A **reserve credit** is the solvency-basis accounting entry the ceding company uses to record a reduction of reserves due to the use of reinsurance. On a reinsured policy, the insurer first establishes a policy reserve in the usual manner. Then the insurer in effect reduces that reserve amount by recording a reserve credit that offsets a portion of the reserve.

Most states restrict the situations in which an insurer in the United States is entitled to take reinsurance reserve credits. Under certain reinsurance agreements, when the reinsurer assumes a portion of the insurer's risk, the reinsurer establishes reserves for some of the reinsured portion of the risk. Under solvency-basis accounting, the ceding company uses a reserve credit to record the reduction of reserves due to the use of reinsurance. Because taking reserve credits can improve an insurer's financial condition, insurers seek to cede risks to reinsurers that meet the specified requirements for reserve credit.

Key Terms and Concepts

reserves
actuarial assumption
actuary
statutory accounting records
GAAP accounting records
internal accounting records
tax accounting records
contractual reserves
noncontractual reserves
claim reserves
reserve valuation method
gross reserve valuation method
gross reserves
net reserve valuation method
net reserves
modified reserve valuation
    method

modified reserve
prospective reserve valuation
    method
present value of
    future benefits
net single premium
present value of future
    net premiums
retrospective reserve
    valuation method
accumulated value of
    net premiums
accumulated cost of
    insurance
policy premium
    method (PPM)
reserve strengthening

Key Terms and Concepts (*continued*)

reserve destrengthening
provision for adverse
   deviation
released reserve
net level premium approach
surplus strain
surplus relief

net GAAP reserves
reinsurance
reinsurer
ceding company
retention limit
reserve credit

Endnotes

1. David B. Atkinson and James W. Dallas, *Life Insurance Products and Finance: Charting a Clear Course* (Schaumburg, IL: The Society of Actuaries, 2000), 366.

2. Ibid.

Chapter 5

Accounting for Liabilities Other Than Reserves

OBJECTIVES

After reading this chapter, you should be able to

- Identify three classifications of policyowner dividend liabilities

- Demonstrate how an insurer accounts for common types of dividend payout options

- Recognize the accounting methods for various nonforfeiture options

- Calculate the amount of a death benefit payment

- Recognize an insurer's typical liabilities other than reserves and benefit payments

*I*n Chapter 4, we discussed how insurers account for their various reserves. This chapter continues our discussion of an insurer's liabilities. An insurer uses most of its income to meet its liabilities—that is, its current and future obligations to policyowners. These obligations include the payment of the following contractual obligations:

- Declared policyowner dividends

- Nonforfeiture options

- Death benefit payments

- Supplementary contract payments

Accounting for an insurer's liabilities also encompasses accounting for premiums paid in advance, premium deposits, debt obligations, expenses due or accrued, premium suspense accounts, and stockholder dividends. We discuss these additional liabilities at the end of the chapter.

Policyowner Dividend Liabilities

Dividends to a mutual insurer's owners and to owners of participating policies are typically known as *policyowner dividends*. A **policyowner dividend** is the portion of an insurer's surplus that is paid to participating policyowners and is considered a partial refund of the policy premium that was not needed by the insurer for policy expenses. **Policyowner dividend liabilities** represent all policyowner dividends that have been declared by an insurer's board of directors, but which have not yet been paid to policyowners.

Annual dividends on participating policies are generally payable on policy anniversaries after a policy has been in force for one or more years. The total amount of policyowner dividends payable in each upcoming year is contingent upon the number of policies still in force on their anniversary dates. For this reason, the amount of policyowner dividends payable that an insurer reports in the U.S. Annual Statement or Canadian Annual Return is an estimate provided by the insurer's actuaries. The insurer does not know what its experience will be until after the end of the year. Also, the insurer cannot determine the exact amount of a policyowner dividend until after December 31 because policyowner dividends typically are declared payable at a future date. A policyowner dividend declared in 2002, for example, typically will not be paid to participating policyowners until sometime in 2003.

The insurer records accounting entries for the total dollar amount of all policyowner dividends being applied under each dividend payout option. After paying a dividend or applying it under an option, the insurer updates its dividend record to provide a detailed history of each policy's dividend transactions. The insurer uses this information to

- Prepare summaries of dividend transactions by state and province for financial reporting purposes

- Prepare lists by policy number and branch office for tracing dividend disbursements in case a policyowner should question whether he or she was sent a dividend

- Facilitate audits by regulatory authorities

- Report interest credited on policyowner dividends for income tax purposes

On U.S. GAAP-based financial statements, an insurer estimates the present value of all future policyowner dividends as a component of policy reserves for certain bundled whole life insurance products. However, for U.S. statutory accounting purposes, the insurer estimates its policyowner dividend liabilities for the next year only. Insurers report the total of their policyowner dividend liabilities on the Liabilities page of the U.S. Annual Statement. In a separate exhibit, insurers list the dollar amounts of policyowner dividends that policyowners have applied under each dividend payment option. Insurers in the United States also disclose the methods used to determine the amount of policyowner dividend liabilities under each payment option. An insurer's liabilities for policyowner dividends include (1) dividends due and unpaid, (2) dividends payable in the following year, and (3) dividend accumulations. We discuss dividend accumulations later in this chapter.

Policyowner Dividends Due and Unpaid

Policyowner dividends due and unpaid are those dividends that were declared by an insurer's board of directors during the year, but that have not yet been paid as of the current financial statement date. An insurer must establish a liability for policyowner dividends due and unpaid whenever the policyowner has earned the dividend but has not yet received it or applied it to a dividend option. Amounts recorded in the liability account *Policyowner Dividends Due and*

Unpaid apply to the current year. These dividends have met all the criteria for payment, and the exact dollar amount of the dividends is known.

Although an insurer's board of directors can declare a policyowner dividend at any time, policyowner dividends are payable on all in-force policies on the policy anniversary date. Under statutory accounting, insurers in the United States typically report the entire projected dollar amount of the policyowner dividend as a liability on the U.S. Annual Statement. Under GAAP, however, the insurer typically reports only that portion of the estimated policyowner dividend that applies to the current reporting period. Keep in mind, however, that there are many exceptions to these typical reporting requirements.

Policyowner Dividends Payable in the Following Year

Policyowner dividends payable in the following year, also called *apportioned dividends*, are the estimated amount of all policyowner dividends that an insurance company's board of directors has declared that are payable in the following calendar year or policy year. Amounts in the liability account *Policyowner Dividends Payable in the Following Year* apply to the following year. In this case, the exact amount of the insurer's liability is unknown because the payment of a policyowner dividend depends upon whether the policy is in force on its anniversary date, which occurs after the U.S. Annual Statement date.

Policyowner Dividend Payment Options

Five applications, called **policyowner dividend payment options** or *dividend payment options*, enable participating policyowners to select the manner in which they want their policyowner dividends disbursed. Policyowners can choose to have their policyowner dividends:

- Paid in cash

- Applied to reduce the premium due on the policy

- Left with the company to accumulate at interest

- Applied to purchase paid-up additions (PUAs) to the policy

- Applied to purchase one-year term insurance

Under the following circumstances, dividends that a policyowner has applied under a dividend payment option must be paid out to a policyowner or beneficiary:

- Withdrawal of dividend accumulations by the policyowner

- Surrender of paid-up additions for their cash surrender value by the policyowner

- Termination of the policy by surrender, by death, or as a paid matured endowment

Insurers routinely record accounting entries for the payment of accumulated dividends held under an option and the cash surrender values of paid-up additions. Such transactions typically involve the insurer's *Cash* account. Figure 5-1 summarizes the accounting treatment of these common dividend payout options.

Figure 5-2 presents a simplified diagram of the process for recording and paying policyowner dividends.

Nonforfeiture Options

When a life insurance policy lapses—that is, the policyowner stops paying premiums—the basic insurance contract terminates, except for those rights that the policyowner has under any nonforfeiture options. **Nonforfeiture options** are the various ways in which a policyowner may apply the cash value of a life insurance policy or an annuity if the contract lapses. **Nonforfeiture values** are the benefits that the insurer guarantees to a policyowner if the insurance contract lapses. Nonforfeiture options may take one of three basic forms: (1) cash surrender, (2) reduced paid-up insurance, or (3) extended term insurance. The following sections present the accounting procedures for these nonforfeiture options.

Cash Surrender

When a policyowner has elected the cash surrender value option, insurance protection stops and the insurer calculates the cash surrender value owed to the policyowner. The insurer then remits this amount to the policyowner, and the company has no further obligation under the policy. A typical accounting entry to record the surrender of a life insurance policy is as follows:

FIGURE 5-1. Policyowner Dividend Payout Options.

POLICYOWNER DIVIDENDS PAID IN CASH

When a policyowner elects to receive a dividend in cash, an insurer typically updates the dividend record and records the appropriate accounting entries upon payment of the policyowner dividend. A typical accounting entry to record the payment of a policyowner dividend is:

    Policyowner Dividends Paid in Cash xxx
            Cash xxx
        To record the cash payment of policyowner dividends.

POLICYOWNER DIVIDENDS APPLIED TO PAY PREMIUMS

When a policyowner uses a dividend to reduce a policy premium, the insurer deducts the policyowner dividend from the premium due to determine the amount owed by the policyowner. The insurer records the accounting entry on the policy anniversary date. The policyowner can receive any excess dividend in cash or apply the remainder to another dividend payment option. To record policyowner dividends applied to pay premiums due, the basic accounting entry is:

    Policyowner Dividends Applied to Premiums xxx
            Premium Income xxx
        To record the application of a policyowner dividend to pay a current premium.

POLICYOWNER DIVIDEND ACCUMULATIONS

Dividend accumulations result when a policyowner elects to leave policyowner dividends on deposit at interest with the insurer. To record dividend accumulations, the insurer establishes a liability for dividend accumulations and for the accrued interest on dividend accumulations. Most insurers record the policyowner dividend and its accrued interest on the policy anniversary date—that is, the date on which the dividend becomes payable—provided that policy premiums have been paid to that date. A typical entry to record a policyowner's election to allow dividends to accumulate at interest with the insurer is:

    Policyowner Dividends Applied to Dividend Accumulations xxx
            Dividend Accumulations xxx

        To record policyowner dividends applied to accumulate with the insurer at interest.

Note that this accounting entry records the initial deposit of the dividend. Separate accounting entries would record the interest earned on the dividends.

POLICYOWNER DIVIDENDS APPLIED TO PURCHASE PAID-UP ADDITIONS (PUAs)

When a policyowner uses a dividend to purchase paid-up insurance, the insurer determines the amount of additional insurance purchased. The insurer then adds a rider to the basic policy to indicate the additional insurance coverage or treats the paid-up insurance as a separate policy. A typical accounting entry to record dividends applied to buy PUAs is:

    Dividends to Purchase PUAs xxx
            Single Premiums for PUAs xxx
        To record dividends applied to purchase paid-up additions.

Note that *Single Premiums for PUAs* is a type of premium income account.

POLICYOWNER DIVIDENDS APPLIED TO PURCHASE ONE-YEAR TERM INSURANCE

This policyowner dividend payout option is commonly called the *fifth dividend option*. The entry to apply policyowner dividends to one-year term insurance is similar to that for paid-up additions, as shown below:

    Dividends to Purchase One-Year Term Insurance xxx
            Single Premiums for One-Year Term
            Insurance xxx
        To record dividends applied to purchase one-year term insurance.

In Canada, applications of either of the last two policyowner dividend payout options are known as *bonus additions*. The insurer usually records payments for paid-up additions and one-year term insurance separately to facilitate accounting for tax and financial reporting purposes.

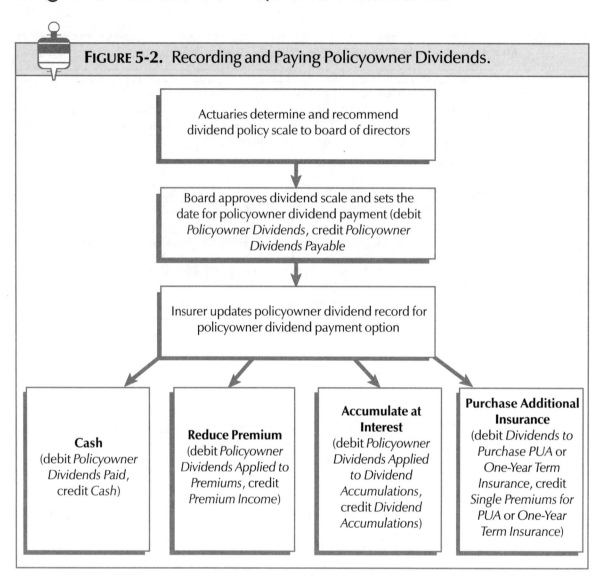

FIGURE 5-2. Recording and Paying Policyowner Dividends.

Actuaries determine and recommend dividend policy scale to board of directors

Board approves dividend scale and sets the date for policyowner dividend payment (debit *Policyowner Dividends*, credit *Policyowner Dividends Payable*)

Insurer updates policyowner dividend record for policyowner dividend payment option

Cash
(debit *Policyowner Dividends Paid*, credit *Cash*)

Reduce Premium
(debit *Policyowner Dividends Applied to Premiums*, credit *Premium Income*)

Accumulate at Interest
(debit *Policyowner Dividends Applied to Dividend Accumulations*, credit *Dividend Accumulations*)

Purchase Additional Insurance
(debit *Dividends to Purchase PUA* or *One-Year Term Insurance*, credit *Single Premiums for PUA* or *One-Year Term Insurance*)

Surrenders Paid—Life Insurance...........xxx
Cash.....................…........................xxx
To record a life insurance policy cash surrender.

The debit to *Surrenders Paid—Life Insurance* typically decreases the insurer's surplus because it immediately increases benefits paid, thereby reducing net income. However, a change in the liability for policy reserves occurs simultaneously. As a result, the net effect on surplus is very small or slightly positive because the decrease in surplus from the payment is offset by an increase in surplus resulting from the reserve released, as shown in Figure 5-3.

FIGURE 5-3. Cash Surrender and Surplus.

Suppose a policyowner surrenders a policy with a cash surrender value of $3,200, and the reserve released for this policy totals $3,400. In this case, there is a $200 increase in surplus, all other factors remaining equal. Recall, however, that insurers do not usually make accounting entries each time transactions affect policy reserves. Therefore, the changes caused by the reserve released (shown in the simplified balance sheet below) will not be recorded until the insurer's actuaries calculate actual reserves at the end of the accounting period.

Balance Sheet

Assets (Cash)	Liabilities
-$3,200	-$3,400

Capital and Surplus (Surplus)
+ $200

Policy loans, dividends, and paid-up additions affect a policy's cash surrender value. If a policy loan is outstanding, the insurer deducts from the settlement the amount of the loan plus any accrued interest to the date of surrender and reduces the cash payment accordingly. If the policyowner had left dividends to accumulate with the insurer, the amount payable to the policyowner would be the cash surrender value plus the amount of the dividend accumulations and their accrued interest. If paid-up additions apply to a surrendered policy, the insurer adds the surrender value of these additions to the cash surrender value of the policy. Figure 5-4 shows how an insurer calculates the total amount payable to this policyowner upon surrender of a life insurance policy.

Reduced Paid-Up or Extended Term Insurance

Because the treatment of reduced paid-up and extended term insurance is similar, we discuss these two nonforfeiture options together. Under the reduced paid-up or extended term insurance nonforfeiture options, the policy's nonforfeiture value is applied as a premium to purchase paid-up term or extended term insurance, paid-up whole life insurance, or paid-up endowment insurance for the policyowner. When a policy continues under one of these options, with no dividend accumulations or policy loans outstanding, the insurer need not make an accounting entry. The transaction is simply a transfer

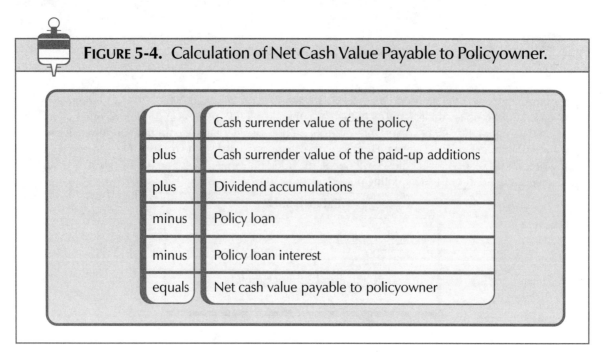

FIGURE 5-4. Calculation of Net Cash Value Payable to Policyowner.

	Cash surrender value of the policy
plus	Cash surrender value of the paid-up additions
plus	Dividend accumulations
minus	Policy loan
minus	Policy loan interest
equals	Net cash value payable to policyowner

of the policy's reserve liability from a premium-paying classification to a paid-up insurance classification. The insurer makes accounting entries only if there were dividend accumulations or an outstanding policy loan at the time of surrender. The insurer also converts the policyowner master file from premium-paying status to paid-up status. A simplified flowchart summarizing the procedure for recording nonforfeiture benefits is presented in Figure 5-5.

Death Benefit Payments

A **death claim** is a request for payment upon the death of the insured, under the terms and conditions of a life insurance policy. Payments on supplementary contracts are typically called **contractual payments**. In this section, we discuss accounting and financial reporting for death benefit payments and contractual payment liabilities associated with life insurance policies. Because the amounts of death benefit payments and contract payments are often quite large, cooperation between an insurer's claims and accounting functions is critical to timely and accurate claims settlement. Many insurance companies record accounting entries for death benefit payments upon approving of the claim. Typical accounts used to record and report death benefit payments include *Death Benefit Payments*, *Death Claims Paid*, or *Claim Settlements*.

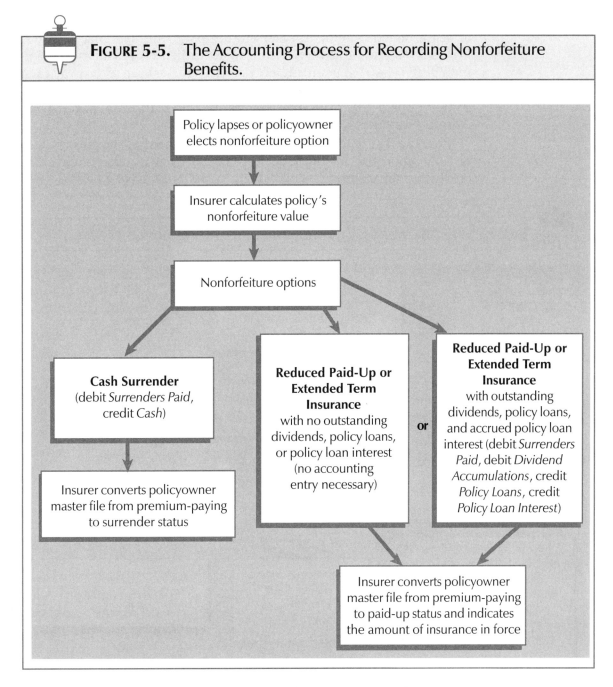

FIGURE 5-5. The Accounting Process for Recording Nonforfeiture Benefits.

If the policy's beneficiary elects a settlement option, the insurer records the accounting entry as soon as it establishes the amounts and conditions of the settlement contract. However, some companies establish a liability for a death benefit payment when they receive notice of the death claim. Moreover, an insurance company that has reinsured the risk will simultaneously establish an asset for amounts due from reinsurance companies for outstanding claims for death benefit payments. In the following sections, our discussion of death benefit payments refers to ordinary life insurance policies. Figure 5-6 shows an overview of the death benefit payment process, including typical accounting entries that an insurer records at each step of the process. Insurers in the United States list the total liability for unpaid life insurance claims on the *Liabilities* page of the Annual Statement.

Most life insurance policies provide for payment of the policy's face amount upon the insurer's death. Some life insurance policies also provide annuity benefits, endowment benefits, or have a provision or

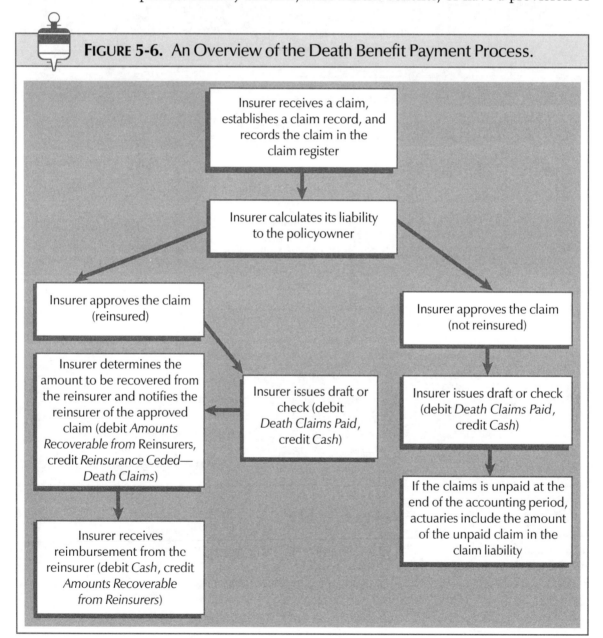

FIGURE 5-6. An Overview of the Death Benefit Payment Process.

Insurer receives a claim, establishes a claim record, and records the claim in the claim register

Insurer calculates its liability to the policyowner

Insurer approves the claim (reinsured)

Insurer approves the claim (not reinsured)

Insurer determines the amount to be recovered from the reinsurer and notifies the reinsurer of the approved claim (debit *Amounts Recoverable from* Reinsurers, credit *Reinsurance Ceded— Death Claims*)

Insurer issues draft or check (debit *Death Claims Paid*, credit *Cash*)

Insurer issues draft or check (debit *Death Claims Paid*, credit *Cash*)

If the claims is unpaid at the end of the accounting period, actuaries include the amount of the unpaid claim in the claim liability

Insurer receives reimbursement from the reinsurer (debit *Cash*, credit *Amounts Recoverable from Reinsurers*)

rider for accidental death and dismemberment (AD&D) benefits. Universal life insurance products may provide a benefit larger than the policy's face amount. In sum, an insurer can make other adjustments to the amount payable to a policy beneficiary. For this reason, the actual amount of death benefit payable often differs from the policy's face amount. The amount of an insurer's liabilities for claims reported in the financial statements usually equals the aggregate amount of all claims. Through debits and credits to other accounts, such as a *claims clearing account*, the insurer makes adjusting entries to the aggregate claim amount. Examples of adjustments that affect the amount of proceeds payable under death benefits payable are listed in Figure 5-7.

Adjustments to the face amount of a policy do not necessarily appear in an insurer's accounting records. Instead, the insurer makes some adjustments directly to the face amount and includes the effect of these adjustments in the debit to *Death Benefit Payments*, for example, by product type. Sometimes the age of the insured is misrepresented in the policy application and this mistake is not discovered until after the death of the insured. In such cases, a reduction in the policy's death benefit requires no separate accounting

FIGURE 5-7. Calculation of Death Benefits Payable.

Items that an insurer can *add* to the policy's face amount include	Items that an insurer can *subtract* from the face amount include
• Return of premiums that have been paid in advance for periods beyond the next policy anniversary • Return of the balance on deposit in a premium deposit fund • Paid-up additions that have been purchased by the policyowner • Policyowner dividends currently payable but not yet paid • Policyowner dividends left with the insurer to accumulate at interest • Policy loan interest paid in advance, but not yet earned by the insurer • Interest paid on delayed claims	• Outstanding policy loans • Accrued policy loan interest at the date of death • Premiums due and unpaid if death occurs during the grace period • Accrued or unpaid premiums (deducted by some companies)

entry. Likewise, an insurer does not have to record a separate accounting entry for the settlement of paid-up additions.

Insurers must also adjust the face amount in case of an insured's suicide within the suicide exclusion period. The amount of the death benefit payable in such cases is typically limited to a return of premiums. If an insurer denies a claim presented during the contestable period because of misrepresentation or fraud in the policy application, the policy is considered to be void from its inception. In this case, the insurer must refund all premiums. A typical accounting entry to record this refund of premiums is as follows:

> **Premium Income** xxx
>   **Cash** xxx
> **To record the refund of a policy premium due to misrepresentation or fraud.**

Waiver-of-Premium Benefits

Most life insurance policies contain a waiver-of-premium rider. The **waiver-of-premium benefit** provides premium payments to keep a life insurance policy in force should the insured become disabled and incapable of earning income to pay the premium. Upon the disability of the insured, an insurer waives the premium due on the life insurance policy according to the terms of the rider. The insurer does not receive cash for the premium, as it would if the insured were able to make ongoing premium payments. However, the insurer still credits *Premium Income* for the amount of the premium waived. By waiving the premium, the insurer also incurs an expense because the insurer is in effect "paying" the policy premium. A typical accounting entry to record this transaction is as follows:

> **Waiver-of-Premium Benefits—Ordinary** xxx
>   **Premium Income** xxx
> **To record the payment of a waived premium.**

The insurer thus credits a revenue account as though the premium had been paid in cash. Insurers in the United States include unpaid settlement contract installments and unpaid disability benefits provided by life policies with the life insurance claim liability on the U.S. Annual Statement. Insurers in Canada typically record accounting entries for premiums waived as a result of disability to a contra account because the Canadian Annual Return excludes these amounts from premium income. Recall from Chapter 3 that a contra account is an account that has a normal balance that is the opposite of its companion account.

Supplementary Contract Payments

Typically, a **supplementary contract**, also known as a *settlement contract*, arises from the election of a settlement option by a life insurance beneficiary. Upon the death of the insured, a life insurance beneficiary can elect to receive a series of payments. Figure 5-8 provides an example of the accounting treatment for a supplementary contract.

Liabilities Other Than Reserves and Benefit Payments

In this section, we discuss a number of liabilities that we have not covered to this point. Many liabilities consist of money that the insurer owes for goods and services. Insurers typically also disclose these liabilities in the U.S. Annual Statement and the Canadian Annual Return.

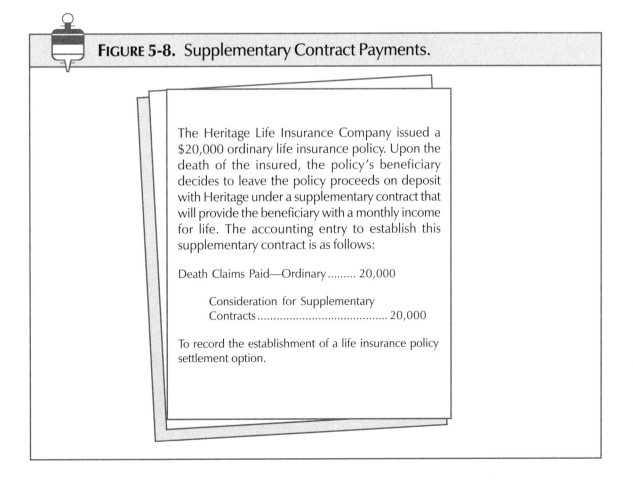

FIGURE 5-8. Supplementary Contract Payments.

The Heritage Life Insurance Company issued a $20,000 ordinary life insurance policy. Upon the death of the insured, the policy's beneficiary decides to leave the policy proceeds on deposit with Heritage under a supplementary contract that will provide the beneficiary with a monthly income for life. The accounting entry to establish this supplementary contract is as follows:

Death Claims Paid—Ordinary 20,000

      Consideration for Supplementary
      Contracts 20,000

To record the establishment of a life insurance policy settlement option.

Premiums Paid in Advance

An insurer reports a liability for **premiums paid in advance**, also called *advance premiums*, when a policyowner pays a premium in one accounting period for coverage that does not begin until the next policy anniversary. Keep in mind that the *Premiums Paid in Advance* liability account differs from the *Unearned Premium Reserves* liability account—which represents amounts paid in an earlier accounting period for coverage that extends into a later accounting period, but not beyond the policy anniversary date. The liability for premiums paid in advance appears on U.S. GAAP, Canadian GAAP, and U.S. statutory financial statements.

Premium Deposits

Premium deposits are amounts that an insurer's policyowners leave on deposit with the insurer to pay for future premiums. Premium deposits apply to more than one future accounting period and are frequently discounted. Although these amounts are available to the insurer now, the insurer will not apply them to premium income until the premium is due. Instead, the insurer credits these funds to *Premium Deposits*, a liability account. Because premium deposits represent future premiums, the insurer does not consider the entire amount as premium income during the current accounting period. The insurer only credits *Premium Income* for the amount of the current premium. The liability for premium deposits appears on U.S. GAAP, Canadian GAAP, and U.S. statutory financial statements.

Debt Obligations

When we discussed an insurer's invested assets in Chapter 2, we saw that insurers purchase large amounts of bonds. Sometimes, however, an insurer issues bonds or enters into other arrangements in which the insurer is a borrower rather than an investor. Bonds that an insurer issues are liabilities to the insurer. Under GAAP, liabilities are commonly divided in a manner similar to that of assets: between short-term (current) and long-term (noncurrent). Recall that *short-term liabilities* are those that generally come due within 12 months. *Long-term liabilities* are those that a company incurs over time, so they cross several accounting periods. Under GAAP, an insurer accounts for interest and principal on short-term and long-term debt separately. Short-term and long-term liabilities are not as clearly differentiated under statutory accounting practices, however.

Expenses Due or Accrued

An insurer estimates its liability for expenses due or accrued for those goods and services it has received but for which the insurer has not yet paid as of the reporting date. Recall that incurred or paid expenses are expense accounts on the income statement and due or accrued expenses are liability accounts on the balance sheet. The following sections briefly discuss an insurer's primary expenses due or accrued.

General Expenses

The liability account *General Expenses Due or Accrued* represents the monetary value of those goods or services an insurer has already received but not yet paid for, as of the financial reporting date. Insurers must exercise a considerable amount of judgment to determine the amount of this liability. For Annual Statement purposes, insurers in the United States report as liabilities any expenses due and accrued from

- Salaries and wages incurred but not yet paid

- Contributions to employee benefit plans

- Professional and service fees

- Utility services used

- Investment expenses

Recall that, under U.S. GAAP, an insurer classifies specified policy-related costs as an asset account—*Deferred Acquisition Costs*—and amortizes these costs over a specified time.

Agents' Commissions Due or Accrued

A **commission** is monetary compensation paid to a sales producer, usually expressed as a percentage of the gross premiums paid by customers. In accounting entries, commissions are usually classified as agents' commissions. Agents' commissions are a significant expense for insurers. An agent's commission is considered due or accrued when the insurer receives a premium too late in the accounting period to process the commission payment to the agent. Commissions generally accrue only on premiums received. Most insurers maintain a separate file for each agent to track unpaid but owed agents' commissions and report the cumulative amount to a liability account such as *Agents' Commissions Due or Accrued*.

Taxes, Licenses, and Fees Due or Accrued

The liability account *Taxes, Licenses, and Fees Due or Accrued* includes (1) items billed but not yet paid, such as business or agent licenses, (2) amounts payable but not yet billed, such as property taxes on real estate, and (3) estimates of amounts still owed for premium taxes, which are levied on premiums collected during the year.

Premium Suspense Accounts

The accounting entry to record an insurer's receipt of a premium typically includes a debit to *Cash*. However, the insurer may not be able to determine immediately the credit entry to offset the debit to *Cash*. In such situations, many insurers use premium suspense accounts. In insurance accounting, a **suspense account** is an account that is used to record transactions that cannot be credited immediately to a specified account. Specifically, a **premium suspense account** is a liability account used to record transactions that are intended as premiums but which the insurer cannot accept as income until a particular event occurs.

Theoretically, upon policy issue, there is little need for a suspense account. However, many insurers initially suspense all insurance premiums. These insurers typically use premium suspense accounts for premium payment amounts that are (1) renewal premiums, (2) different from the amounts in the insurer's records, or (3) lacking critical information, such as a policy number. A typical accounting entry to account for such transactions is as follows:

> Cash xxx
>   Premium Suspense xxx
> **To record receipt of a premium payment that cannot be immediately recorded to a premium income account.**

After the particular event occurs—for example, the insurer confirms the correct amount or policy number—the insurer can then debit the premium suspense account and credit a revenue account for the premium amount, as follows:

> Premium Suspense xxx
>   Premium Income xxx
> **To record the application of a suspensed premium as an actual premium.**

Dividends to Stockholders Declared and Unpaid

Besides the liability for policyowner dividends on participating life insurance policies, stock insurance companies must also establish a liability for cash dividends to stockholders as of the date that the insurer's board of directors declares the dividend. The insurer charges dividends to stockholders directly to a surplus account, such as *Dividends to Stockholders*. A typical accounting entry to record a declared dividend is as follows:

> Dividends to Stockholders xxx
>   Dividends to Stockholders Declared and Unpaid xxx
>
> To record the declaration of cash dividends to stockholders.

Upon paying the dividend, the insurer would make the following accounting entry:

> Dividends to Stockholders Declared and Unpaid ... xxx
>   Cash xxx
>
> To record the payment of cash dividends to stockholders.

Key Terms and Concepts

policyowner dividend

policyowner dividend
    liabilities

policyowner dividends due
    and unpaid

policyowner dividends payable
    in the following year

policyowner dividend
    payment options

dividend accumulations

bonus additions

nonforfeiture options

nonforfeiture values

death claim

contractual payments

waiver-of-premium benefit

supplementary contract

premiums paid in advance

premium deposits

commission

suspense account

premium suspense account

premiums paid in advance

premium deposits

commission

suspense account

premium suspense account

Chapter 6

Accounting for Capital and Surplus

OBJECTIVES

After reading this chapter, you should be able to

- Describe the major capital and surplus accounts of life insurers

- Explain how changes in assets and liabilities affect an insurer's surplus

- Discuss the effect on surplus of changes in the market value of invested assets

- List several internal and external sources of capital and surplus for life insurance companies

Recall that the difference between an insurer's assets and its liabilities is represented by owners' equity in the basic accounting equation. For insurance companies, owners' equity accounts consist primarily of capital accounts and surplus accounts. In insurance accounting, **capital** is the money that an insurer's owners have invested in the insurer. Typical capital accounts include *Common Stock*, *Preferred Stock*, and *Additional Paid-in Capital*. In insurance accounting, **surplus** is the amount that remains when an insurer subtracts its liabilities and capital from its assets. Typical surplus accounts include *Special Surplus* and *Unassigned Surplus*.

The prudent and effective management of capital and surplus is critical to an insurer's solvency and profitability:

- **Solvency** generally is the ability of a company to meet its financial obligations on time.

- **Profitability** is the degree to which a company is successful in consistently generating returns to its owners.

Insurers must operate profitably to provide their owners—whether they are stockholders or policyowners—with a fair return on their investment. An insurer's capital and surplus must also be able to provide for unexpected events. In this respect, capital and surplus are the insurer's ultimate defense against the threat of insolvency. **Insolvency** is the inability of a company to pay its financial obligations on time. The insurer's capital and surplus must therefore be sufficient to cover not only the monetary amount that exceeds its contractual reserves during the year, but also to continue to meet the minimum statutory surplus requirements established by insurance regulators. When insurance regulators, rating agencies, and independent financial analysts measure the financial soundness of an insurance company, they pay special attention to the condition of the insurer's capital and surplus accounts.

In this chapter, we present the concepts of capital and surplus, discuss an insurer's primary capital and surplus accounts, describe the internal and external sources of capital and surplus, and summarize the disclosure of capital and surplus on the U.S. Annual Statement and the Canadian Annual Return. In our discussion, we use the term *capital and surplus* to mean the insurer's total owners' equity, whether calculated under GAAP or statutory accounting. Recall that insurers in the United States use capital accounts for U.S. GAAP- and statutory-based financial statements and surplus accounts to satisfy statutory reporting requirements. When we discuss *capital* or *surplus* separately, we are focusing on specific attributes of either capital accounts or surplus accounts, but not both.

Essential Concepts of Capital and Surplus

Recall that, although capital accounts are found on the balance sheets of companies in many industries, surplus accounts are specific to the insurance industry. Legal requirements and accounting standards generally prescribe the types and proper valuations of assets and liabilities that can determine the amount of an insurer's surplus. Insurers in the United States use various capital and surplus accounts for statutory reporting purposes. However, when insurers prepare U.S. GAAP-based financial statements, they assign much of their surplus to an account called *Retained Earnings*. The total in *Retained Earnings* represents the cumulative amount of a company's earnings that has been kept in the company over time to finance the company's ongoing operations. Like *Retained Earnings*, capital and surplus accounts are classified as owners' equity in the basic accounting equation, which follows:

$$\text{Assets = Liabilities + Owners' equity}$$

More commonly, however, the basic accounting equation for insurers is shown in the following forms:

$$\text{Assets = Liabilities + Capital and Surplus}$$
$$\text{OR}$$
$$\text{Assets = Liabilities + Capital + Surplus}$$

The second form of the equation is especially useful when we discuss capital accounts and surplus accounts separately. Figure 6-1 explains further the relationships among capital and surplus in the basic accounting equation.

Again, for U.S. statutory accounting purposes, surplus is the difference between an insurer's *admitted* assets and its liabilities. For insurers in Canada, surplus is simply the difference between an insurer's assets and its liabilities, because admitted assets and non-admitted assets are U.S.-specific terms. Figure 6-2 lists several key capital and surplus accounts that differ under U.S. GAAP and statutory accounting practices. Note that stock insurance companies in the United States have capital accounts such as *Common Stock* and *Preferred Stock* under both GAAP and statutory accounting.

FIGURE 6-1. Capital and Surplus in the Basic Accounting Equation.

An insurer's capital equals its assets, net of its liabilities and surplus. Similarly, an insurer's GAAP surplus equals its assets, net of its liabilities and capital, as follows:

Capital = Assets – Liabilities – Surplus
Surplus = Assets – Liabilities – Capital

For statutory reporting purposes, insurers in the United States include only admitted assets in the calculation of surplus, as follows:

Surplus = Admitted Assets –
Liabilities – Capital
(U.S. statutory accounting practices)

Capital Accounts

Stock insurers typically use capital accounts to record the issue or purchase of their own stock. The following sections describe an insurer's typical capital accounts under GAAP, which include *Common Stock, Preferred Stock, Additional Paid-in Capital*, and *Retained Earnings.* We also discuss two other accounts that directly affect an insurer's total capital and surplus: *Treasury Stock* and *Unrealized Gains and Losses.*

FIGURE 6-2. Capital and Surplus Accounts Under U.S. GAAP and Statutory Accounting Practices.

U.S. GAAP	U.S. Statutory Accounting
Additional Paid-In Capital	Gross Paid-In and Contributed Surplus
Retained Earnings	Special Surplus
Retained Earnings	Unassigned Surplus

Common Stock Issuance

A typical accounting entry to record the issuance of common stock at par value is a debit to *Cash* and a credit to *Common Stock*, as follows:

Cash xxx	
Common Stock xxx	
To record the issuance of common stock at par value.	

The following balance sheet illustrates the effects of issuing and selling common stock:

Balance Sheet. Issuance and sale of common stock.	
Assets Increase in *Cash* from sale of common stock	**Liabilities** No change
	Capital Increase

Preferred Stock Issuance

Recall from Chapter 2 that preferred stock, a type of equity security that represents ownership in a corporation, usually provides for the payment of a fixed periodic dividend that is paid before any dividends can be paid on the corporation's common stock. The general characteristics of preferred stock as a source of financing are the same for stock insurance companies as they are for any other stock company and, in many ways, the same as the characteristics of common stock. Proceeds from the sale of preferred stock increase the issuing corporation's capital and surplus accounts just as do proceeds from the sale of common stock. A typical accounting entry to record the issuance of preferred stock at par value is a debit to *Cash* and a credit to *Preferred Stock*, as follows:

Cash xxx	
Preferred Stock xxx	
To record the issuance of preferred stock at par value.	

Issuing preferred stock or common stock requires the issuing corporation to pay transaction costs that reduce the corporation's net proceeds from the sale of the stock. The stock issuer must also plan for dividend payments because owners of preferred stock and owners of common stock expect to receive dividend payments. Dividends on common stock or preferred stock are payable only upon the approval of the issuing corporation's board of directors. Dividends on preferred stock are payable according to a schedule. The board of directors may choose not to declare the payment of a scheduled dividend on preferred stock if the issuing company's circumstances—such as extreme financial distress—warrant such a choice.

Preferred stock is sometimes referred to as a *hybrid* type of security because it has some of the characteristics of debt securities, such as bonds, and some of the characteristics of equity securities, such as common stock. Preferred stock differs from common stock— and is correspondingly similar to debt securities—in two notable respects:

- **A dividend payment schedule**. Dividends on preferred stock have a set dividend payment schedule and are characterized as fixed dividends. **Fixed dividends** are dividend payments that are fixed in both schedule and amount. Unlike debt, however, preferred stock generally has no fixed maturity date.

- **Cumulative dividends**. Usually, dividends on preferred stock are also cumulative. **Cumulative dividends** are a type of preferred stock dividend arrangement in which a company must pay in full any unpaid scheduled dividends on its preferred stock before it may pay any dividends on its common stock. However, a failure to pay dividends on preferred stock is not considered to be a default, as would a failure to pay interest or principal on a bond.

The following balance sheet illustrates the effects of issuing preferred stock:

Balance Sheet. Issuance and sale of preferred stock.	
Assets Increase in *Cash* from sale of preferred stock	**Liabilities** No change
	Capital Increase

Additional Paid-in Capital

If the selling price of the stock issue is greater than the stock's par value, insurers in the United States also credit *Additional Paid-in Capital* (U.S. GAAP) or *Gross Paid-in and Contributed Surplus* (statutory accounting) for the excess of the selling price over the par value, as follows:

Cash xxx	
Common Stock xx	
Additional Paid-In Capital x	
To record the issuance of common stock at greater than par value.	
Cash xxx	
Preferred Stock xx	
Additional Paid-In Capital x	
To record the issuance of preferred stock at greater than par value.	

Because Canadian insurers do not record par value, the accounting entry for the issuance of stock, regardless of selling price, is simply a debit to *Cash* and a credit to *Common Stock* or *Preferred Stock*.

Retained Earnings

Retained earnings are the profits that a corporation holds to reinvest in the business instead of paying the money out in dividends to the corporation's owners. Under U.S. GAAP, only specified transactions can directly increase or decrease the *Retained Earnings* account. These transactions include the amount of gains or losses in the company's operations, dividends paid to stockholders, extraordinary items, prior period adjustments (PPAs), and monetary adjustments that result from changes in accounting procedures. A detailed discussion of these transactions is beyond the scope of this textbook.

Treasury Stock

Treasury stock is stock that an insurer in the United States had previously issued, then later repurchased at market price, with the intention of reselling the stock at a later date. The insurer may resell the stock on a stock exchange or through an employee compensation or pension plan that enables employees to purchase shares of the insurers' stock under specified conditions. If the insurer has no intention of reissuing its treasury stock, then the stock is known as **retired stock**.

Increases in the *Treasury Stock* account ultimately decrease an insurer's total capital because *Treasury Stock* is a type of contra account. Recall that a contra account typically decreases the amount in its companion account. The companion account to *Treasury Stock* is *Common Stock*. The amount of *Additional Paid-In Capital* under U.S. GAAP or *Gross Paid-In and Contributed Surplus* under U.S. statutory accounting equals the difference between (1) the par value of the treasury stock multiplied by the number of shares retired and (2) the purchase price, as follows:

> **Par value × Number of shares – Purchase price = Additional Paid-In Capital**
>
> **Par value × Number of shares – Purchase price = Gross Paid-In and Contributed Surplus**

The cash purchase of treasury stock reduces the insurer's *Cash*, an admitted asset under statutory accounting practices. Because the insurer's liabilities and surplus are not affected by this transaction, the insurer must reduce *Common Stock* to maintain the balance in the basic accounting equation. Statutory requirements often limit the amount of treasury stock to a specified percentage of the insurer's total capital and surplus or total assets. An insurer's treasury stock is listed in the U.S. Annual Statement or Canadian Annual Return.

Unrealized Gains and Losses

Recall that an *unrealized gain (loss)* is the difference between an asset's carrying value in the accounting records and its current market value while the company continues to hold the asset. An invested asset may gain or lose market value while it is being held by the insurer. Because the insurer still holds the asset, it has not yet generated a *realized* gain or loss. However, the value of the asset has changed from the insurer's original purchase price, and this change affects the insurer's overall financial condition as represented on the balance sheet.

Only specified assets, such as the common stocks of publicly traded companies, are reported at market value. For other invested assets, an insurer will decrease the value of an invested asset—through a process known as "writing down"—if the asset declines significantly and the insurer does not reasonably expect the asset to increase in value over time. An insurer reports an unrealized loss if the asset's current value is less than the value recorded in the insurer's accounting records and the decrease in value is expected to be temporary. However, the insurer would report the loss as a realized loss if the decrease in value is other than temporary. Because liabilities are not affected by this transaction, insurers in the United States report the amount of the decrease in an asset's value under its capital and surplus accounts. The insurer decreases the asset's value to its *realizable value*, which is the value of an asset as if it had been sold or had matured, even though the insurer still owns the asset.

If an asset has been written down in value, it cannot be written up in value, even if the market value of that asset recovers. To indicate a permanent adjustment in the book value of an asset, the insurer reports the amount as a realized loss—in other words, as if the asset had actually been sold at a loss—on the income statement. In such circumstances, insurers in Canada debit a loss account and credit a contra asset account. Insurers in the United States debit a realized loss account—such as *Realized Loss on Bonds*—and credit the appropriate asset account—*Bonds*—as follows:

> **Realized Loss on Bonds** xxx
> **Bonds** xxx
> **To write down the value of a permanently impaired bond.**

Surplus Accounts

The following sections summarize an insurer's typical surplus accounts, which include *Special Surplus* and *Unassigned Surplus*.

Special Surplus

For insurers in the United States, **special surplus**, or *special surplus funds*, consists of the part of the insurer's surplus that the insurer's board of directors has set aside to (1) meet unforeseen contingencies or (2) pay for certain extraordinary expenses. Special surplus is also known as *assigned surplus*, *appropriated surplus*, *earmarked surplus*, or *contingency reserves*. Keep in mind that the equivalent accounts for insurers in Canada are liability accounts—such as contingent liabilities, which are established as a cushion against specified events that may occur—not surplus accounts. Amounts in the *Special Surplus* account are not available for distribution to owners, nor do they replace an insurer's obligation to establish liabilities for expected occurrences.

The amount in an insurer's *Special Surplus* can be voluntary or involuntary, depending on statutory requirements. In the case of voluntary special surplus funds, an insurer's board of directors can designate the amount of special surplus. An insurer uses an involuntary special surplus account for a specified purpose. One example of an involuntary special surplus fund in most states is the *Participation in Separate Accounts*, which requires all insurers in the United States to allocate a specified amount of their surplus to provide protection for the separate accounts of their customers. A typical accounting entry that an insurer uses to establish this special surplus fund is

> **Unassigned Surplus** .... **xxx**
> **Participation in Separate Accounts** .... **xxx**
> To establish a special surplus account for separate accounts.

Unassigned Surplus

The *Unassigned Surplus* account under statutory accounting is similar to the *Retained Earnings* account under GAAP in that *Unassigned Surplus* represents the accumulation of income not paid out in dividends. For insurers in the United States, **unassigned surplus**, also called *unassigned surplus funds, divisible surplus,* or *free surplus,* is the total amount of undistributed and unapportioned surplus remaining in the insurance company since the company began operations. Unassigned surplus is available to meet any contingency that arises, including new business, outstanding debt, or the purchase of treasury stock or retired stock. An insurer can also use unassigned surplus to satisfy a contingency which has since exhausted the special surplus fund that the insurer originally established for that contingency or to pay operating expenses when a company experiences a net loss during a year.

Dividends paid to owners are withdrawn from unassigned surplus. An insurer's owners typically prefer to receive more dividends and higher dividends. However, the insurer's ability to declare a dividend on its stock depends on the amount available in its *Retained Earnings* account (GAAP) or *Unassigned Surplus* account (statutory accounting). Ultimately, the more dividends an insurer pays to its owners, the lower the amount of growth possible in *Retained Earnings* or *Unassigned Surplus*. States may require approval for an insurer to pay dividends to its owners. For example, state regulations could limit stockholder dividends to a proportion of the insurer's *Unassigned Surplus* so the insurer can maintain an adequate level of surplus.

Before declaring dividends to its owners, an insurance company's board of directors uses *Unassigned Surplus* as one factor in determining the dividend amount. Two primary factors in determining the amount of *Unassigned Surplus* available for distribution to an insurer's owners are (1) the amount of business that the insurer writes and (2) the contractual agreements that the insurer may have, such as loan agreements that might affect its future financial situation. Recall that, once a stockholder dividend has been declared, it becomes a liability to the insurer.

Internal Sources and Uses of Capital and Surplus

An *internal source* of capital and surplus is one that increases an insurer's capital and surplus by financial transactions that originate in the insurer's core business operations. An insurer's typical internal sources of capital and surplus include

- Net income from a net gain from operations or from the sale of invested assets

- An increase in admitted assets (U.S. statutory accounting only)

- Destrengthening reserves

Keep in mind that an insurer's internal *uses* of capital and surplus have the opposite effect of the insurer's sources of capital and surplus. That is, uses of capital and surplus decrease an insurer's capital and surplus accounts. Internal uses of capital and surplus may result from

- A net loss from operations or from the sale of invested assets

- A decrease in admitted assets (U.S. statutory accounting only)

- Strengthening reserves

The following sections briefly describe an insurer's internal sources of capital and surplus.

Net Income

Recall that net income is total revenues *minus* total expenses. The primary source of an insurer's surplus is net income, which includes gains from both (1) insurance operations and (2) the sale of assets:

- *Gains from insurance operations.* Insurers can increase surplus when they earn profits from their operations because revenues are higher than expenses.

- *Gains from the sale of assets.* Insurers also increase net income and ultimately surplus by selling invested assets for a gain. A **gain** is any income that an insurer obtains from a transaction outside its core business operations. Similarly, a **loss** occurs when an insurer loses money on a transaction that is outside the insurer's core business operations. Insurers in Canada amortize the gains on the sale of their invested assets through income, which ultimately affects surplus.

Increases in Admitted Assets (U.S. Only)

Recall that, in the U.S. Annual Statement, admitted assets are those assets that are permitted to be reported on the Assets page. Suppose an insurer purchases office furniture (a nonadmitted asset) and pays cash (an admitted asset) for this purchase. This transaction ultimately results in a decrease in the insurer's surplus under U.S. statutory accounting practices because the value of the insurer's admitted assets decreases.

Thus, for insurers in the United States, an increase in the insurer's nonadmitted assets cannot increase its surplus. Instead, increasing nonadmitted assets typically occurs when an insurer exchanges admitted assets for nonadmitted assets, and this exchange results in a decrease in the insurer's admitted assets. On the other hand, selling furniture for cash replaces a nonadmitted asset—furniture—with an admitted asset—cash. This transaction ultimately increases an insurer's capital and surplus because the insurer exchanges a nonadmitted asset for an admitted asset. Figure 6-3 shows the relationship between an insurer's admitted assets and nonadmitted assets and its capital and surplus.

Destrengthening Reserves

Sometimes the amount of an insurer's reserves changes, not as a result of the insurer's core business operations, but because the insurer changes its *reserve valuation basis*, which is the method the insurer uses to value reserves. Generally, a decrease in an insurer's contractual reserves increases the insurer's surplus. On the other hand, an increase in the insurer's contractual reserves usually decreases the insurer's surplus. A detailed discussion of these effects is beyond the scope of this textbook.

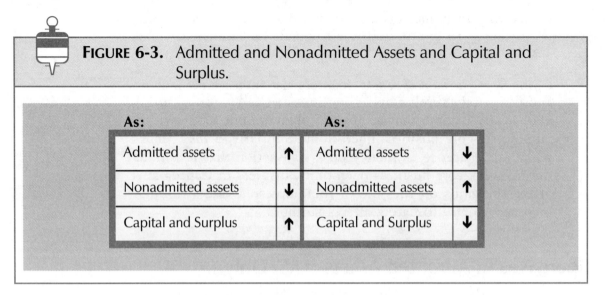

FIGURE 6-3. Admitted and Nonadmitted Assets and Capital and Surplus.

External Sources and Uses of Capital and Surplus

An *external source* of capital and surplus means that an insurer's capital and surplus are increased by financial transactions that originate outside an insurer's core business operations. Typical external sources of capital and surplus for insurers include

- Ceding insurance risk to a reinsurer

- Selling in-force business

- Selling stock

- Issuing surplus notes

Keep in mind that external *uses* of capital and surplus, which have the opposite effect of an insurer's sources of capital and surplus, decrease an insurer's capital and surplus accounts. External uses of an insurer's capital and surplus include

- Assuming insurance risk from a ceding company

- Purchasing in-force business

- Purchasing the company's own stock

- Repaying surplus notes

The following sections highlight common external sources of capital and surplus for life insurance companies.

Reinsurance

An insurer can reduce surplus strain and control its exposure to risk by reinsuring the covered amount that exceeds the company's retention limit for that type of policy. Recall from Chapter 4 that *reinsurance* is a transaction between two insurance companies in which the reinsurer (the assuming company) agrees to take on some of the insurance risks of the insurance company that issued the policy (the ceding company). Also recall that *surplus strain* is the decrease in an insurer's surplus caused by the high first-year costs and the reserving requirements associated with the insurer's new products. An insurer's *retention limit* is the maximum amount of coverage per life that the insurer will keep at its own risk, without ceding a portion of the risk to a reinsurer.

Under the terms of some types of reinsurance agreements, if a ceding company transfers part of its risk to a reinsurer, then the ceding company maintains contractual reserves to cover only the amount of the risk that it has retained. Because this use of reinsurance allows a ceding company to establish a lower amount of contractual reserves than it normally would, the ceding company's surplus is higher than it would have been without reinsurance. In Chapter 4, we discussed the use of reserve credits to reduce reserves. However, some types of reinsurance agreements require the ceding company to maintain contractual reserves, so a reserve credit is not part of the agreement. Only those reinsurance agreements that enable a ceding company to maintain a lower amount of contractual reserves than it would have maintained without reinsurance provide an external source of surplus for the ceding company.

Selling In-Force Business or a Subsidiary

An insurer can also increase its capital and surplus through the sale of in-force business. If the difference between the in-force business sold and the reserves released on that business produces a gain, then an insurer's surplus increases. The insurer can use a particular type of reinsurance known as **assumption reinsurance**, which is a reinsurance agreement designed to transfer blocks of existing insurance business permanently and entirely from one insurance company to another.

Under assumption reinsurance, the assuming company bears the entire legal obligation formerly borne by the ceding company.

Consequently, the ceding company no longer maintains the contractual reserves for that block of in-force business. Instead, the assuming company assumes all obligations and ownership rights associated with the line of business or block of insurance policies. The ceding company transfers assets and liabilities to the assuming company. An assumption reinsurance transaction may result in a gain or loss. If the value of the transferred assets is less than the liabilities released, then a gain results and capital increases, as shown in the following balance sheet:

Balance Sheet. Results of an assumption reinsurance transaction.	
Assets Decrease	**Liabilities** Decrease
	Capital Increase

Issuing Stock

Recall that a stock insurer can increase its capital by issuing common stock or preferred stock. In turn, the insurer decreases its capital and surplus by retiring or purchasing its own stock. Insurers in the United States separate the value of the stock they issue into two components: (1) par value and (2) additional paid-in capital. The par value of the stock is recorded in an account such as *Common Stock* or *Preferred Stock*. The difference between a stock's par value and its original selling price is recorded in *Additional Paid-in Capital* (U.S. GAAP) or *Gross Paid-in and Contributed Surplus* (statutory accounting). Assets and capital both increase as a result of issuing stock and bonds. Insurers in Canada no longer report the par value of stock.

Issuing Surplus Notes

A **surplus note** is a special type of unsecured debt security, issued only by insurance companies, that has characteristics of both traditional equity securities and traditional debt securities. Surplus notes are issued with a fixed schedule of payments of principal and interest. Typically, the insurer is permitted to make scheduled payments of interest and principal on a surplus note only with the approval of the insurance commissioner in the insurer's state of domicile.

The entire proceeds obtained from surplus notes constitute new capital. The proceeds from a sale of surplus notes are recorded by one accounting entry showing an increase to the issuing company's capital and surplus accounts, and another entry that increases the *Cash* account, with no change in the insurer's liabilities, as illustrated in the following balance sheet:

Balance Sheet (Solvency basis). Issuance and sale of surplus notes.	
Admitted Assets Increase in *cash* from sale of surplus notes	**Liabilities** No change
	Surplus Increase in surplus

Insurers in the United States include surplus notes under *Surplus* for statutory reporting purposes. In other words, issuing surplus notes increases an insurer's surplus, not its liabilities, under statutory accounting practices. By issuing surplus notes, an insurer's ability to pay claims on a timely basis is improved, because the increases in both *Cash* and *Surplus* strengthen the insurer's balance sheet. However, under U.S. GAAP, insurers report surplus notes as liabilities, not surplus.

Changing Corporate Form

In response to increased competition and technological advances in the financial services industry, some insurers have changed their corporate form. To grow and increase capital, insurers can restructure their corporate form through

- **Mergers, acquisitions, takeovers, and divestitures**. Mergers and acquisitions have the effect of combining formerly independent corporations. From the perspective of the acquired company, an acquisition or merger is a takeover or divestiture. From the perspective of the acquiring company, the transaction is an acquisition.

- **Holding company structures**. Insurers use holding company relationships to facilitate various types of corporate affiliations.

- **Demutualization**. *Demutualization* is the process of converting a mutual insurance company to a stock insurance company. By demutualizing, a mutual insurer gains access to capital sources available to stock insurers.

- **Mutual holding company**. The creation of a holding company whereby policyholders own a mutual insurer through the mechanism of an upstream holding company is an interim step to full demutualization.

- **Financial holding company**. The primary impact of the United States federal legislation known as the *Gramm-Leach-Bliley (GLB) Act* of 1999 is that the traditionally separate components of the financial services industry—banks, securities firms, and insurance companies—now can structurally converge under the umbrella of a federally chartered *financial holding company*. The financial holding company can engage in a statutorily provided list of financial activities that formerly were divided by regulation.

Figure 6-4 summarizes an insurer's typical internal and external sources and uses of capital and surplus.

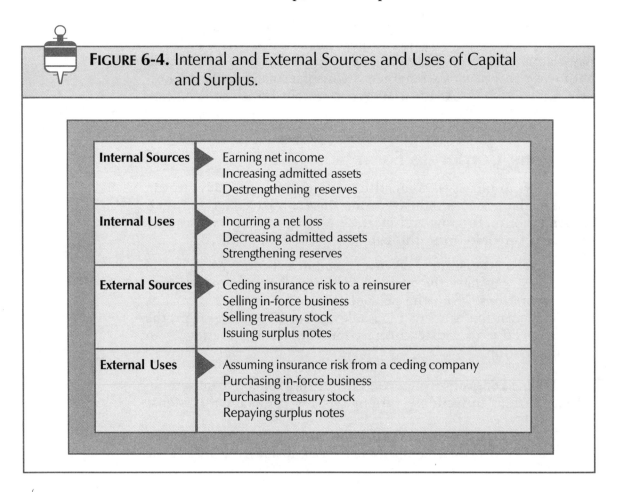

FIGURE 6-4. Internal and External Sources and Uses of Capital and Surplus.

Internal Sources	▶ Earning net income Increasing admitted assets Destrengthening reserves
Internal Uses	▶ Incurring a net loss Decreasing admitted assets Strengthening reserves
External Sources	▶ Ceding insurance risk to a reinsurer Selling in-force business Selling treasury stock Issuing surplus notes
External Uses	▶ Assuming insurance risk from a ceding company Purchasing in-force business Purchasing treasury stock Repaying surplus notes

Reporting Changes in Capital and Surplus Accounts

An insurer's capital accounts typically do not change in value as a result of the insurer's core business operations. Rather, they change as a result of a specific transaction, such as the insurer's issue of stock or repurchase of treasury stock. On the other hand, the amount of an insurer's surplus can and does change daily as a result of the company's insurance operations. Although the insurer does not record accounting entries each time surplus is affected, it does prepare accounting entries at the end of the accounting period to report the aggregate effect of these changes on surplus. The amount of an insurer's surplus changes because of internal and external sources and uses of capital and surplus, as outlined in this chapter, as well as changes in reserves, which we discussed in Chapter 4. The following sections describe how insurers in the United States and Canada report changes in surplus.

United States

Life insurance companies in the United States have three main surplus accounts under statutory accounting:

- *Gross Paid-In and Contributed Surplus*

- *Special Surplus*

- *Unassigned Surplus*

   Gross paid-in and contributed surplus is the aggregate amount paid above the par value for shares of an insurer's stock. Recall that *Gross Paid-In and Contributed Surplus* is the statutory equivalent account to *Additional Paid-In Capital* under U.S. GAAP. Thus, the insurer's issue of additional shares of stock or purchase of outstanding shares of its own stock affects the net annual change in the *Gross Paid-In and Contributed Surplus* account in consecutive reporting periods.

   Changes in an insurer's investments in separate accounts affect the insurer's surplus. If total assets exceed total liabilities for the separate accounts, then the amount of excess increases the insurer's surplus. On the other hand, if total liabilities exceed total assets for the separate accounts, the excess decreases surplus. Also, insurers in the United States use write-in lines to make any necessary capital and surplus adjustments, such as corrections of previous years' results from operations. A detailed discussion of these adjustments is beyond the scope of this textbook.

Canada

The Liabilities page of the Canadian Annual Return separates owners' equity accounts into policyholders' equity and shareholders' equity. Policyholders' equity includes (1) a participating account for participating life insurance policies, (2) a nonparticipating account for mutual companies, and (3) a currency translation account. Shareholders' equity includes (1) capital stock, (2) contributed surplus, (3) retained earnings, and (4) a currency translation account. The *Capital Stock* account is similar to the *Common Stock* and *Additional Paid-In Capital* accounts under U.S. GAAP.

Until 1994, a Canadian insurer's surplus consisted of both *Appropriated Surplus and Unappropriated Surplus*. These terms are equivalent to *Special Surplus* and *Unassigned Surplus* for insurers in the United States. However, the Minimum Continuing Capital and Surplus Requirements (MCCSR), which we discuss in Chapter 10, now incorporate amounts that an insurer previously categorized as *Appropriated Surplus*. For insurers in Canada, the method of reconciling surplus changes between reporting years on the Canadian Annual Return is similar to that used on the U.S. Annual Statement. However, keep in mind that, under Canadian GAAP, insurers do not differentiate between admitted assets and nonadmitted assets.

Key Terms and Concepts

capital
surplus
solvency
profitability
insolvency
fixed dividends
cumulative dividends
retained earnings
treasury stock
retired stock

special surplus
unassigned surplus
gain
loss
assumption reinsurance
surplus note
demutualization
gross paid-in and
    contributed surplus

Chapter 7

Accounting for Revenues

OBJECTIVES

After reading this chapter, you should be able to

- Identify the main sources of revenues for life insurance companies

- List the basic objectives of accounting for premium income

- Recognize the accounting entries associated with typical premium income transactions

- Differentiate among types of investment income generated by different invested assets

- Recognize the accounting entries associated with typical investment income transactions

- Differentiate between gross investment income and net investment income

- Discuss the presentation of premium income and investment income on the U.S. Annual Statement and Canadian Annual Return

C hapter 7 shifts our focus from items that appear on the balance sheet to revenue accounts, which appear on the income statement. Recall that revenues are amounts earned from a company's sales of products and/or services to its customers. **Revenue accounts**, sometimes called *income accounts*, are the accounts used to record and report a company's revenues. The term *income* can have several meanings in accounting. For example, net income is a company's revenues less expenses. In general, however, income is synonymous with revenue in that income is the money earned from the sales of a company's products and/or services.

When to recognize revenues is important in accounting and financial reporting. In accounting terminology, **recognition** is the process of recording a transaction in a company's accounting system as an asset, liability, owners' equity, revenue, or expense account. Under GAAP, insurers report revenues according to the realization principle and accrual-basis accounting. The **realization principle** states that a company should recognize revenues when they are earned, rather than when they are received, so long as a legal and reasonable expectation exists that the company's customer will remit payment in full. Under **accrual-basis accounting**, a company records revenues when they are earned and expenses when they are incurred, even if the company has not yet received the revenues or paid the expenses. Under **cash-basis accounting**, a company recognizes revenues or expenses only when the company receives or disburses cash. Thus, the realization principle does not apply under cash-basis accounting. Accrual-basis accounting is used under GAAP. Because the statutory accounting hierarchy follows the GAAP hierarchy, insurers who file the U.S. Annual Statement, which is prepared under statutory accounting practices, also use accrual-basis accounting.

This chapter discusses the accounting and financial reporting requirements associated with an insurer's typical revenue accounts. Although the actual account names can and do vary among insurance companies, most revenue accounts have self-explanatory names, such as *Premium Income—Life Insurance* and *Investment Income—Common Stock Dividends*. Insurers typically have two primary sources of revenues: (1) premium income and (2) investment income. Besides premium income and investment income, an insurer's income statement also includes other sources of revenue from its core business operations. Examples of these revenue sources include

- Considerations for structured settlements and supplementary contracts

- Premiums for reinsurance assumed

- Fee income for brokerage services, management services from scparate (segregated) account business, and third-party administrator (TPA) services

- Management fees related to the side funds associated with universal life insurance and variable annuity products

A discussion of these additional sources of revenue is beyond the scope of this textbook.

Income Classifications

Under accrual-basis accounting, insurers typically classify income according to when the income is (1) earned, (2) due, and (3) collected. Figure 7-1 summarizes these income classifications. Keep in mind that these terms are not an important distinction under Canadian GAAP, because insurers in Canada recognize an entire premium received as premium income.

Figure 7-2 compares these types of income.

FIGURE 7-1. Income Classifications Under Accrual-Basis Accounting.

The accounting entries that accompany each income classification assume that the reporting period runs from January 1 through December 31 and that the financial reporting date is December 31.

Collected income is the amount of income received in cash during a reporting period, including certain adjustments. For example, premiums received for the reporting period from January 1 through December 31 constitute collected income.

Unearned income, a subset of collected income, is income that has been collected but not yet earned. For example, an **unearned premium** is that portion of the insurance premium received in one period, but applicable to the insurance coverage to be provided in the following period but before the next policy anniversary date. Unearned premiums usually apply to group life insurance premiums and not to individual life insurance premiums or annuity considerations.

Deferred income is premium income for insurance policies due after the U.S. Annual Statement reporting date but before the next contract anniversary date. The classification of *deferred premiums* applies to premium payments made more frequently than annually.

Figure 7-1. Income Classifications Under Accrual-Basis Accounting (continued).

Uncollected income is income that is due before December 31, but which the insurer has not received as of December 31. Recall that *uncollected premiums* primarily refer to individual life insurance premiums and annuity considerations, whereas ***due premiums*** generally refer to group life insurance premiums.

Accrued income is income that the insurer has already earned but which is receivable after the end of the current reporting period. *Accrued income* typically applies to interest or dividends on an insurer's invested assets, because such income is legally collectible. Premium income typically is not classified as accrued income.

For insurers in the United States, ***nonadmitted income*** is uncollected income that is overdue for more than a specified period—such as three months to two years—as prescribed by state insurance laws. By classifying long overdue income as nonadmitted income, an insurer is implying that it is not certain whether this income will ever be collected.

Premium income includes premium payments that an insurer receives for individual life insurance, group life insurance, annuity considerations, considerations paid on supplementary contracts, and premiums for reinsurance assumed. Because most of an insurer's revenues consist of policy premiums, the insurer must be aware of the external and internal factors that directly affect the nature, amount, and timing of its premium income. Figure 7-3 discusses several typical external and internal factors affecting premium income.

The following sections discuss accounting for premium income and investment income.

Premium Accounting

Premium transactions usually comprise the largest number of an insurer's accounting entries. **Premium accounting**, sometimes called *policy accounting*, includes maintaining detailed accounting records and reports of insurance transactions. Examples of insurance transactions include premium billing and collections and accounting for agent commissions, policy claims, policy loans, and policy dividends.

Different insurers use many different types of premium accounting systems, reflecting differences in company organization, management preferences, and lines of business. For example, some

FIGURE 7-2. Income Classifications Compared.

Type of Income	Received?	Earned?	Account Classification
Collected	Yes	Yes*	Revenue
Unearned	Yes	No	Liability
Uncollected	No	Yes	Asset
Accrued	No	Yes	Asset
Deferred**	No	No	Asset
Nonadmitted (statutory accounting practices only)	No	Yes	Nonadmitted asset

*Collected income may have both an earned and an unearned portion.

***Deferred Premiums* is an asset account established to offset the overstated reserve liability.

insurance companies centralize premium collections at the home office. Other companies have regional offices or several collection centers throughout their marketing areas. Nonetheless, the primary function of a premium accounting system is to record premium income as soon as the insurer earns it.

The most important objectives of an insurer's premium accounting system are to

- Bill for premiums before their due date, with sufficient lead time between the billing and due dates

- Record the receipt of premiums in the premium accounting system

- Classify premium income by product type, jurisdiction, and other specified categories so the insurer can use the data to calculate taxable income and prepare financial statements by line of business or product

- Accept premium payments after the expiration of the grace period under circumstances acceptable to the insurer

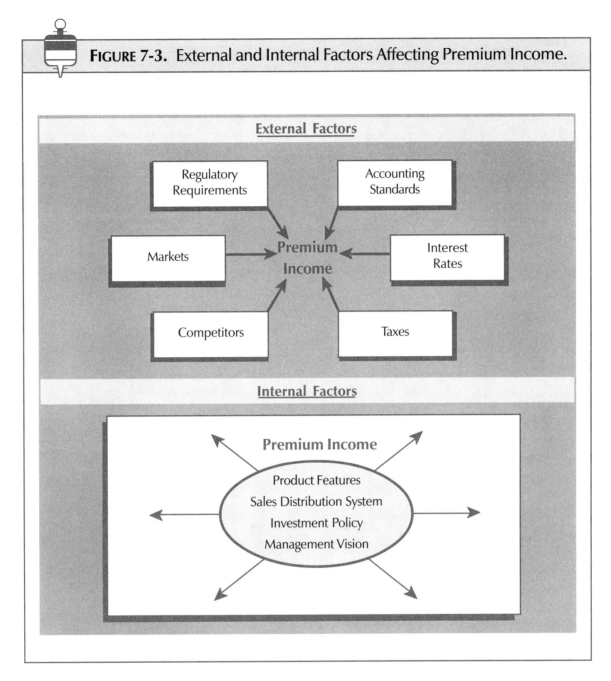

FIGURE 7-3. External and Internal Factors Affecting Premium Income.

- Terminate a policy or change the policy from a premium-paying status to a specified nonforfeiture option, if the policyowner has not paid the premium

Figure 7-4 depicts the general process of premium accounting at policy issue and policy renewal.

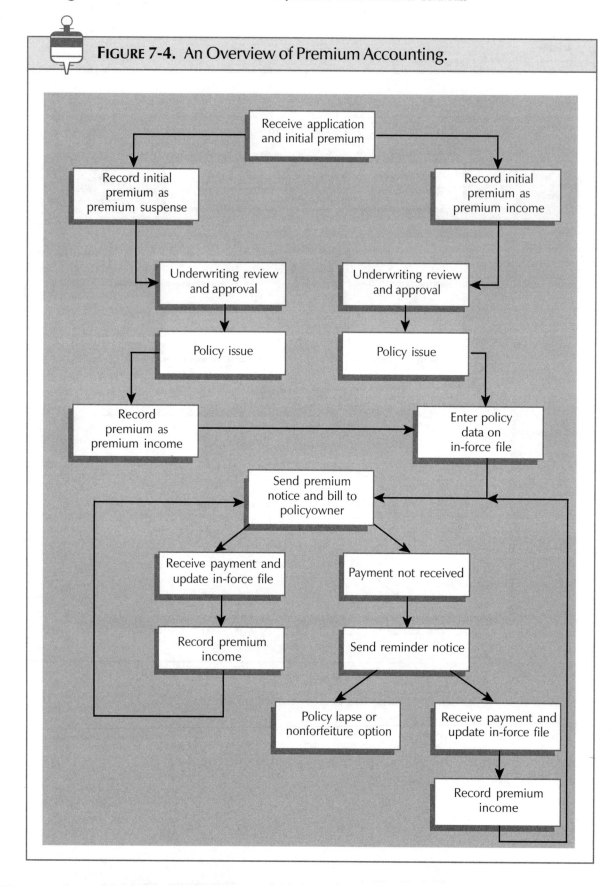

FIGURE 7-4. An Overview of Premium Accounting.

Premium Accounting Entries

Generally, the receipt of policy premiums increases an insurer's revenues and assets. Premiums are usually deposited in the insurer's bank account upon receipt. This practice provides for good accounting and makes the funds available for investment. The accounting treatment of premium income directly affects an insurer's financial reports, particularly the cash flow statement, which reports all changes in cash from normal business operations. By monitoring policy premium receipts, an insurer can generate premium notices and past-due warnings, as well as change a policy's status from premium paying to non-premium paying.

The basic accounting entry to record a collected premium on most insurance products is a debit to *Cash*, an asset account, and a credit to a revenue account, such as *Premium Income*:

> **Cash** xxx
> **Premium Income** xxx
> **To record the receipt of premium income.**

Recall from Chapter 5 that some insurers initially suspense premiums upon receipt by debiting *Cash* and crediting *Premium Suspense* in the first accounting entry. *Premium Suspense* is the liability account that represents the insurer's obligation (1) to provide insurance coverage if the policy is approved or (2) to return the initial premium to the applicant if the policy is declined. Upon approving the policy, the reason for holding the premium in suspense no longer applies. In this case, a second accounting entry is made to debit *Premium Suspense* and credit *Premium Income*. Note that the combined effect of these two accounting entries is a debit to *Cash* and a credit to *Premium Income*. If the insurer declines to issue a policy, then it must return the initial premium to the applicant. A typical accounting entry to record the return of the initial premium, which was originally deposited in a suspense account, is a debit to *Premium Suspense* and a credit to *Cash*, as follows:

> **Premium Suspense** xxx
> **Cash** xxx
> **To record the return of an initial premium to the applicant.**

Figure 7-5 depicts an example and a timeline that shows the relationship among collected, uncollected, and unearned premiums.

Accounting for Policy Loan Interest

Two additional sources of revenue associated with insurance products are (1) interest income on policy loans and (2) policy dividends

FIGURE 7-5. Timeline: Collected, Uncollected, and Unearned Premiums.

The Hermitage Life Insurance Company offers a life insurance policy that has a quarterly mode of premium payment. Premium payments are due on March 1, June 1, September 1, and December 1 of each year. Assume that the reserves are calculated using the *midterminal reserve method*, which is the average of the policy's terminal reserve for the previous policy year and the terminal reserve for the current policy year. Also assume that the policy anniversary date is June 1. The policyowner paid the entire annual premium on June 1, 2001, which advanced the policy's paid-to date to June 1, 2002.

On its balance sheet dated December 31, 2001, Hermitage records an unearned premium for this policy. Recall that an unearned premium is a liability because the insurer has not yet provided the insurance coverage. On the other hand, an uncollected premium is an asset, because it represents amounts that Hermitage expects to receive. In this example, because the paid-to date occurs after December 31, 2001, there is no uncollected (due) premium. Suppose the paid-to date were December 1, 2001, and Hermitage did not receive the premium payment by that date. In this case, Hermitage records an uncollected premium on its December 31, 2001, balance sheet.

Below are two timelines that show the relationship among collected premiums, uncollected premiums, and unearned premium.

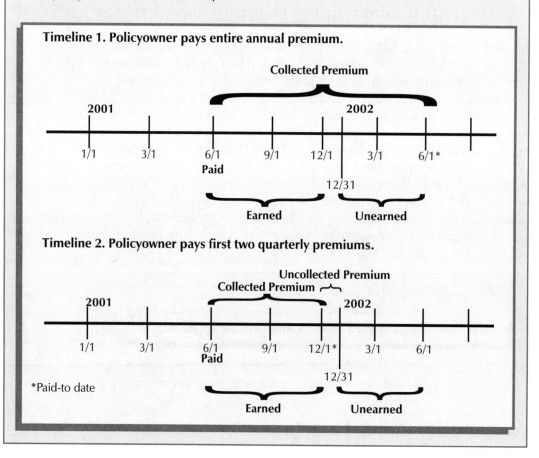

applied to premiums for additional insurance. Recall that we discussed accounting for premium income with respect to policy dividend options in Chapter 5. Ordinary life insurance policies that build cash value usually have a policy loan provision. Policy loan interest is usually payable on the policy anniversary date. If the insurer does not receive interest on the policy loan by this date, then the insurer adds the amount of the unpaid interest to the policy loan balance, provided the policy's cash value is sufficient to cover both the principal and interest on the loan. A typical accounting entry to record the insurer's receipt of policy loan interest consists of a debit to *Cash* (an asset account) and a credit to *Policy Loan Interest* (a revenue account), as follows:

Cash xxx	
Policy Loan Interest xxx	
To record the receipt of policy loan interest.	

Financial Reporting Requirements— Premium Income

An insurance company complies with accounting and financial reporting requirements by classifying its premium income and investment income according to the following product types:

- Life

- Accident and health

- Credit life

- Annuities (individual and group)

Thus, insurers typically credit one of several revenue accounts according to the revenue source and the type of policy. For example, when a policyowner remits a renewal premium for a life policy, the journal entry might include a credit to an account entitled *Premium Renewals—Life*. This specific account enables the insurer to identify this source of revenue by revenue type (premium income) and by line of business (life insurance).

To report premium income on an accrual basis, insurers in the United States separately identify premiums as (1) collected premiums, (2) uncollected premiums, (3) deferred premiums, and (4) unearned premiums. The example in Figure 7-6 illustrates the mechanics of reporting premium income on an accrual basis. The purpose of this calculation is to determine the amount of premium income that the insurer *earned* during the fiscal year, which generally differs from the amount of premium income the insurer *collected* during the same period.

FIGURE 7-6. Accrual-Basis Premium Income.

Example

Premium income collected	$1,000,000
+ Gross deferred and uncollected premiums at the end of the current period	250,000
− Gross deferred and uncollected premiums at the end of the previous period	(100,000)
− Unearned premiums at the end of the current period	(175,000)
+ Unearned premiums at the end of the previous period	100,000
= Accrual-basis premium income	$1,075,000

Investment Income Accounting

Recall that investment income consists of the earnings a company receives on its invested assets. However, investment income does not include gains or losses—whether realized or unrealized—associated with an insurer's invested assets. Interest on bonds and mortgages, rental income on real estate, and dividends on stock are typical sources of an insurer's investment income. Income earned on an insurer's invested assets is usually the insurer's second largest source of revenues, after premium income. In some insurance companies, the amount of investment income exceeds that of premium income. Figure 7-7 summarizes the forms of investment income that insurers earn on various invested assets.

Accounting Entries for Investment Income

Account titles for investment income vary among insurers. For example, one insurer may have an account called *Bond Interest Income*. Another insurer may call this account *Interest Income—Bonds*. Regardless of the account title, an insurer records in its investment income accounts all income earned and received on the invested assets that it owns. A typical accounting entry to record the receipt of investment income is a debit to *Cash*, an asset account, and a credit to one or more investment income accounts, which are revenue accounts, as shown in Figure 7-8.

FIGURE 7-7. Types of Investment Income.

Invested Asset	Interest Income	Dividend Income	Rental Income
Stocks	No	Yes	No
Bonds	Yes	No	No
Mortgages	Yes	No	No
Policy loans	Yes	No	No
Real estate	No	No	Yes

Keep in mind that insurers in the United States report the amount of earned investment income that has not yet been received under *Investment Income Due and Accrued*, an asset account. When the insurer receives the earned income, it records the amount of the income as a debit to *Cash* and a credit to *Investment Income Due and Accrued*.

Financial Reporting Requirements— Investment Income

Insurers also recognize investment income on an accrual basis for financial reporting requirements. **Gross investment income** is the accrual-basis amount of income that represents the total amount of income the insurer actually earned during the reporting year, before deducting expenses. **Net investment income** is the amount of investment income that remains after deducting expenses and amortization from the insurer's gross investment income. Insurers in the United States must show on the U.S. Annual Statement the amount of net investment income generated during the year by investment type and category of income. Insurers in Canada also show investment income on an accrual basis on the Canadian Annual Return.

Canadian GAAP differs from U.S. GAAP and statutory accounting practices in the treatment of realized gains and losses on invested assets. Under Canadian GAAP, if an insurer sells a bond that matures in 10 years, the total gain or loss is amortized into income on the income statement over the 10 years. The insurer would report the

FIGURE 7-8. Investment Income Accounting Entries.

INTEREST INCOME ON BONDS

Cash.................xxx

     Interest Income—Bonds..... xxx

To record interest income received on bonds owned by the insurer.

INTEREST INCOME ON MORTGAGES

Cash.................xxx

     Interest Income—Mortgages xxx

To record interest income received on mortgages owned by the insurer.

RENTAL INCOME ON REAL ESTATE

Cash.................xxx

     Rental Income—Real Estate xxx

To record rental income received on real estate owned by the insurer.

CASH DIVIDENDS ON COMMON STOCK

Cash.................xxx

     Dividend Income—Common Stock.....xxx

To record dividend income received for the common stock owned by the insurer.

unamortized portion of the bond on the balance sheet. Insurers in Canada also itemize the amount of accrued and earned gross investment income from their invested assets, such as bonds, stock, mortgages, real estate, and other revenue sources. By deducting investment expenses and investment taxes from gross investment income, the insurer obtains net investment income.

Key Terms and Concepts

revenue accounts	deferred income
recognition	uncollected income
realization principle	due premiums
accrual-basis accounting	accrued income
cash-basis accounting	nonadmitted income
collected income	premium accounting
unearned income	gross investment income
unearned premium	net investment income

Chapter 8

Accounting for Expenses

OBJECTIVES

After reading this chapter, you should be able to

◉ Identify and differentiate among an insurer's major expenses

◉ Recognize how insurers report expenses in the U.S. Annual Statement and the Canadian Annual Return

◉ Identify the objectives of accounting for agents' commissions

◉ Recognize accounting entries for typical expenses incurred in life insurance companies

◉ Demonstrate an understanding of the purposes of premium taxes, retaliatory taxes, and guaranty-fund assessments

*I*nsurers incur expenses while conducting normal business operations. Recall that an expense is generated when an insurer's assets are used to obtain or support the insurer's revenues during the current reporting period. Contractual benefit payments, which we discussed in Chapter 5, are typically the largest expense for insurers. Thus, life insurance companies allocate a large proportion of every premium dollar for contractual benefits. The remaining portion of every premium dollar must cover the insurer's operating expenses and allow for a profit. Figure 8-1 highlights an insurer's typical expenses.

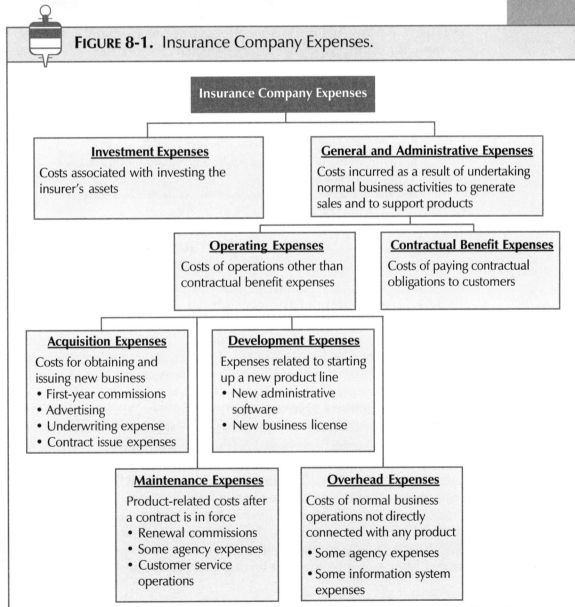

FIGURE 8-1. Insurance Company Expenses.

Insurance Company Expenses

Investment Expenses
Costs associated with investing the insurer's assets

General and Administrative Expenses
Costs incurred as a result of undertaking normal business activities to generate sales and to support products

Operating Expenses
Costs of operations other than contractual benefit expenses

Contractual Benefit Expenses
Costs of paying contractual obligations to customers

Acquisition Expenses
Costs for obtaining and issuing new business
• First-year commissions
• Advertising
• Underwriting expense
• Contract issue expenses

Development Expenses
Expenses related to starting up a new product line
• New administrative software
• New business license

Maintenance Expenses
Product-related costs after a contract is in force
• Renewal commissions
• Some agency expenses
• Customer service operations

Overhead Expenses
Costs of normal business operations not directly connected with any product
• Some agency expenses
• Some information system expenses

Source: Adapted from Susan Conant, *Product Design for Life Insurance and Annuities* (Atlanta: LOMA, © 2001), 41. Used with permission; all rights reserved.

Investment expenses are the costs associated with investing the insurer's assets. Examples of investment expenses include brokerage commissions and administrative fees that insurers pay to buy, hold, and sell their invested assets. *General and administrative expenses* are the costs incurred as a result of the insurer's normal business operations, including both (1) contractual benefit expenses and (2) operating expenses. This chapter focuses on an insurer's typical operating expenses. We also separately discuss several insurance-specific taxes.

Insurers record each type of expense in a specified expense account. When an insurer pays a particular expense, the insurer debits the appropriate expense account and credits *Cash*. Insurers summarize their expenses on the income statement at the end of each reporting period. Insurers typically maintain a separate expense account for each type of operating expense. For example, an insurer may record expenses incurred for public accounting services in an expense account, as follows:

> **Public Accounting Expense .... xxx**
> **Cash .... xxx**
> **To record the payment to a public accountant for financial statement auditing.**

Contractual Benefit Expenses

An insurer's primary liabilities are the contractual reserves and claim reserves maintained to account for the amounts the insurer expects will be needed to pay current and future contractual benefits. When an insurer sells an insurance policy or annuity contract, the insurer becomes legally obligated to pay the benefit amount associated with that product if certain conditions are met. Contractual benefits include death benefits, cash surrenders, disability benefits, and annuity contract payments.

Recall from Chapter 4 that, when an insurer pays a contractual benefit, the reserves associated with that contract are released. A released reserve is a contractual reserve that was originally established in connection with an in-force contract, but which is no longer required. Insurers do not reduce their reserves each time a contractual benefit is paid, however. Instead, when an insurer pays a contractual benefit, the insurer debits an expense account, such as *Death Benefits Paid*, and credits *Cash* for the amount of the payment. At the end of the accounting period, the insurer's actuaries recalculate the reserves required for each block of policies. The insurer then records an accounting entry that shows the changes in reserves.

Operating Expenses

Insurers also incur operating expenses that are similar to those incurred by non-insurance companies. **Operating expenses** are the expenses—other than contractual benefit expenses—that arise in the normal course of conducting business. Operating expenses include:

- Acquisition expenses

- Development expenses

- Maintenance expenses

- Overhead expenses

Although insurers can readily identify the amount of contractual benefits and agent commissions incurred by policy type or line of business, it is more difficult to determine what portion of the insurer's operating expenses applies to a particular line of business. One important aspect of accounting for expenses concerns the allocation of operating expenses. In accounting, to *allocate* an amount is to distribute the amount proportionally among several accounts. The U.S. Annual Statement and the Canadian Annual Return require insurers to allocate operating expenses by lines of business.

A common method of allocating expenses is based on the amount of premium income for each line of business. First, the insurer determines what percentage of total premium income each line of business earned for the reporting period. Next, the insurer multiplies total operating expenses by that percentage to calculate the amount of operating expenses to allocate to each line of business. Keep in mind that, for agents' commissions and other expenses that can easily be attributed to a specified product or line of business, expense allocation is unnecessary. Figure 8-2 shows an example of allocating operating expenses to each line of business for the U.S. Annual Statement.

Acquisition Expenses and Development Expenses

Acquisition expenses are the costs of obtaining and issuing new business. They include advertising expenses, underwriting expenses,

FIGURE 8-2. Operating Expense Allocation Based on Premium Income.

	Ordinary Life	Group Life	Total
Premium income	$10,000	$40,000	$50,000
Percentage of $50,000 premium income	20 percent	80 percent	100 percent
Allocation of $20,000 operating expenses	$4,000	$16,000	$20,000

contract issue expenses, and first-year agent commissions. **Development expenses** are the expenses related to starting a new product line. Development expenses include the costs of new administrative software and new business licenses. Under Canadian GAAP and U.S. statutory accounting practices, expenses are recognized during the reporting period in which they occur. However, under U.S. GAAP, specified costs associated with developing or acquiring a new product can be classified as an asset—*Deferred Acquisition Costs (DAC)*—and expensed over the premium-paying period of the product. We discussed deferred acquisition costs in Chapter 3.

The following sections discuss agent commissions, agent salaries, and reinsurance commissions.

Agent Commissions

Agent commissions are typically an insurer's second largest expense after contractual benefit expenses. Insurers that use agents to sell individual life insurance products typically pay their agents on a commission basis. Regardless of the distribution system used, insurers must have an accounting system that can accurately record and report commissions and salaries incurred in summary form and by line of business or product type. An insurer's income statement typically contains summary information that shows the total amount of commissions earned by and paid to all agents. Detailed activity for each agent's commissions is contained in the insurer's internal accounting records.

The objectives of commission accounting are to

- Calculate the amount of agent commissions payable on each premium an insurer receives

- Record agent commissions payable to each agent

- Establish a clear accounting record from the amount of the premium payment to the commissions earned by and paid to each agent

For financial reporting purposes, a company establishes a control account for each incurred commission expense. A ***control account*** summarizes accounting entries and serves as a control for the monetary amounts of expenses that are reported in a company's financial statements. A typical control account, called *Agents Ledger Control*, includes commissions an insurer owes to agents as well as amounts that agents owe to the insurer. The amount of money owed by an insurer to an agent represents an *account payable*, which is a current liability because the insurer expects to pay the agent within the current accounting period.

The amount of money owed by an agent to an insurer, often called *Agent Balances Due*, is a type of *account receivable.* This account is a short-term asset account, because the insurer expects to receive this amount within the reporting period. Many insurers advance commissions to a new agent during his or her first months with the insurer. Under statutory accounting practices, agent balances due more than a specified length of time are generally a nonadmitted asset for life insurance companies in the United States.

Several types of accounting entries occur frequently in connection with agent commissions. Note, however, that insurers do not typically withhold taxes from agent commissions, although they do withhold taxes from salaried employees, including salaried agents. Figure 8-3 shows several typical accounting entries associated with recording agent commissions.

Some insurance companies also pay commission bonuses to agents for exceeding target production levels. These bonuses usually represent a commission expense for insurers. The accounting entries to record these commission bonuses are similar to the transactions to record commissions earned and paid.

Agent Salaries

Most life insurance companies have a distribution system that relies primarily on commissioned agents. However, some insurers, especially direct response companies and group life insurers, rely

FIGURE 8-3. Accounting for Agent Commissions.

When the Veritable Life Insurance Company's agents earn commissions, Veritable records an accounting entry to show that it has incurred the commission expense and has established a liability for the commissions owed to its agents, as follows:

Commissions Expense xxx

     Agents Ledger Control xxx

To record incurred agent commissions expense.

Upon payment of the earned commission to the agent, Veritable records the following accounting entry:

Agents Ledger Control xxx

     Cash xxx

To record the payment of agent commissions.

The combined effect of the two transactions is an increase in an expense account—*Commissions Expense*—and a corresponding decrease in an asset account—*Cash*.

---

on salaried agents. In most cases, salaried agents are agents to whom an insurer provides financial assistance in establishing a client base. Also included in this group are branch or field office managers to whom the insurer provides both a salary and commission overrides for developing an agency office. Such agents are considered employees of the insurer.

In the case of salaried agents, an insurer is required to withhold payroll taxes, just as the insurer does for other salaried employees. Recall that insurers do not withhold taxes from amounts paid to commissioned agents. A detailed discussion of accounting for payroll is beyond the scope of this textbook. You should know, however, that payroll taxes withheld by an insurer are recorded in liability accounts. These liability accounts represent amounts that the insurer has collected on behalf of a governmental body and thus is obligated to pay. When the insurer pays taxes, the insurer debits the appropriate liability account and credits *Cash*. The effect of paying taxes to a governmental body decreases both the tax liability account and cash. Figure 8-4 shows how an insurer accounts for payments to its salaried agents and other salaried employees.

FIGURE 8-4. Accounting for Agent Salaries.

Suppose a salaried agent at the Yorba Life Insurance Company earns a $1,000 monthly salary. From this salary, $100 must be withheld for federal income taxes, $50 must be withheld for payroll taxes, and $20 must be withheld for state income taxes. Yorba's accounting entry to establish liabilities for federal and state taxes and the amount payable to the salaried agent is as follows:

Salaries Expense	1,000
Federal Income Taxes Payable	100
Payroll Taxes Payable	50
State Income Taxes Payable	20
Salaries Payable	830

To record the establishment of a liability for an agent's salary and the appropriate tax withholdings.

This accounting entry records Yorba's liability for taxes withheld as $170 ($100+$50+$20) and records the salary payable to the agent as $830 ($1,000 – $170). Thus, the amount payable to the agent equals the salary expense minus any withholdings.

When Yorba pays the agent's salary, an appropriate accounting entry is as follows:

Salaries Payable	830
Cash	830

To record the payment of an agent's salary.

When the company then pays the state income taxes withheld from the agent's salary, the appropriate journal entry is as follows:

State Income Taxes Payable	20
Cash	20

To record the payment of state income taxes withheld from an agent's salary.

Some salaried agents receive a year-end bonus for generating new business and maintaining that business. The insurer treats a salaried agent's bonus as part of that agent's salary and withholds the appropriate amounts for tax purposes, as with salary payments. For financial reporting purposes, the insurer maintains separate accounting records for each salaried agent, as well as each agent that receives a combination of salary and commission payments.

Reinsurance Commissions

The use of reinsurance represents another consideration when accounting for commissions. Recall that, in reinsurance transactions, the company that purchases reinsurance is the ceding company and the reinsurer is the assuming company. Commissions that the reinsurer pays to the ceding company are called **reinsurance commissions**, which are payments intended to cover all or part of the ceding company's acquisition costs and other costs related to the reinsured business. In effect, the assuming company pays a commission on this new business, just as any insurer pays a commission to an agent for new business. In such situations, the assuming company pays the commission to the ceding company, rather than to an agent.

If an insurer cedes part of the insurance risk on a block of insurance policies to an assuming company, then the ceding company pays periodic premiums to the assuming company. Besides reimbursing the ceding company for a stated portion of the claims incurred under the reinsurance business, the assuming company usually reimburses the ceding company for agents' commissions, taxes, and other reimbursable expenses under certain reinsurance agreements. Figure 8-5 depicts an example of accounting for reinsurance premiums.

Maintenance Expenses and Overhead Expenses

Maintenance expenses and overhead expenses are other categories of an insurer's operating expenses. **Maintenance expenses** are product-related costs that are incurred after a contract is in force. Renewal commissions paid to agents and ongoing customer service costs are typical maintenance expenses for life insurance companies. **Overhead expenses**, commonly called *overhead costs* or simply *overhead*, are the costs of conducting normal business operations not directly related to a specified product or service. Common examples of overhead expenses include the costs of furniture, telephone service, electricity, research, accounting fees, and other business fees, which are difficult to assign to a specified product.

FIGURE 8-5. Accounting for Reinsurance Premiums.

Suppose the Creekside Life Insurance Company cedes $250,000 of a block of ordinary life policies to Lakeland Re. If the reinsurance treaty specifies a reinsurance premium of $800 and a reinsurance expense allowance of $600, then, to record payment of the reinsurance premium expense, Creekside makes the following accounting entry:

Reinsurance Ceded—First-Year Premium Expense 800

Reinsurance Expense Allowance—Ceded 600

Cash 200

To record the payment of reinsurance premium expense, net of expense allowance.

Lakeland Re records the receipt of the reinsurance premium income as follows:

Reinsurance Expense Allowance—Assumed 600

Cash 200

Reinsurance Assumed—First-Year Premium Income 800

To record the receipt of reinsurance premium income, net of expense allowance.

Taxes, Licenses, and Fees

Taxes, licenses, and fees are generally classified as operating expenses. Life insurance companies pay the same kinds of taxes—such as property taxes and unemployment taxes—that other companies pay. In addition, insurers pay some insurance-specific taxes and assessments. Typically, an insurer's accountants coordinate the company's efforts to minimize its tax liability. These efforts require input from the actuarial, investment, marketing, and sales functions. Typical taxes, licenses, and fees incurred by life insurance companies include:

- Federal income taxes

- Premium taxes

- Municipal taxes in some states

- State or provincial income taxes

- Property taxes

- Foreign insurance department licenses, fees for state examinations, and business licenses

- Guaranty fund assessments

- Payroll taxes

Insurers in the United States and Canada are subject to federal income taxes and state or provincial taxes. Insurers also must comply with laws and accounting regulations that affect corporations, including accounting standards that provide specific guidance concerning income tax accounting. Complying with current laws and regulations is a complex matter for life insurance companies. A full discussion of taxes is beyond the scope of this textbook. The following sections briefly discuss insurance company taxes.

Insurers in the United States

According to the Internal Revenue Service (IRS) definition of a life insurance company in the United States, more than half of an insurer's business during the tax year must come from the issuance of insurance or annuity contracts or the reinsurance of risks underwritten by life insurance companies. In addition, more than 50 percent of the insurer's total reserves must be reserves for life insurance, unearned premiums, and unpaid losses on noncancelable life, accident, or health insurance policies. The IRS categorizes fraternal benefit societies and other similar benefit associations as tax-exempt insurance companies.

It is to an insurer's advantage to comply with the IRS definition of a life insurance or a tax-exempt insurance company because the tax rules and regulations directly address an insurer's unique business operations. A business categorized as a life insurance company for tax purposes can deduct certain insurance-specific items from gross income to determine its tax liability. However, an insurer can meet the definition of a life insurance company according to its state of domicile, but not meet the IRS's stricter definition of a life insurance company for federal income tax purposes. Also, depending on the type of insurance products it offers, an insurer may no longer be allowed the tax treatment accorded to insurers.

Because of different definitions and timing differences, amounts shown on the tax return for various revenues and expenses may not be identical to the amounts reported for those items in the insurer's U.S. Annual Statement or other financial statements for the same accounting period. Thus, the items included in net income and the way net income is calculated varies among statutory accounting, GAAP, and tax accounting.

Because of the nature of the life insurance industry, there are several unique tax deductions for life insurance companies in the United States, including deductions for (1) increases in life insurance company reserves, (2) policyowner dividends, and (3) qualifying as a small life insurance company. Life insurers in the United States determine the amount of income that is subject to federal income taxes by calculating *life insurance company taxable income (LICTI)*, which is the difference between a life insurance company's gross income and its tax deductions. To calculate LICTI, insurers first determine gross income, which includes advance premiums and excludes deferred and uncollected premiums. Gross income is also adjusted for policyowner dividends applied under a dividend option other than cash and premiums waived as a result of disability or applied to purchase supplementary contracts.

Contractual reserves are a key factor in determining an insurer's taxable income. Increases in reserves are deductible from an insurer's gross income. For example, if an insurer's reserves at the beginning of the year are $50 million, and its reserves at the end of the year are $51 million, it has experienced a $1 million increase in reserves. The insurer can then deduct this $1 million difference from its taxable income. The IRS also specifies which insurance company expenses are deductible from gross income to obtain taxable income. Expenses that are tax deductions from LICTI include three main categories, as follows:

- *Expenses associated with obtaining income,* including claims, paid or accrued policy dividends and experience rating refunds, agent commissions and insurance expenses, and other benefits associated with life insurance and annuity contracts

- *Increases in specified reserves* (described above)

- *General corporate deductions,* including depreciation on long-term assets and amortization of bond premiums

Small insurance companies in the United States—that is, those with less than $500 million in assets calculated under tax rules—also qualify for an additional deduction, called the *small life insurance company deduction.* A company that is eligible for the small life insurance company deduction calculates gross income and subtracts deductible expenses from gross income to obtain tentative LICTI. *Tentative LICTI* is the amount of gross income minus deductible expenses before subtracting the small life insurance company deduction, excluding income from non-insurance operations. The insurer must include in gross income only those revenues that arose from its life insurance operations, including investment income to support company liabilities and specified reinsurance transactions. The small life insurance company deduction enables a qualifying insurer to deduct up to 60 percent of its tentative LICTI (up to a maximum $1,800,000), to determine its taxable income according to a specified formula.

Insurers in Canada

Life insurers in Canada comply with the *Canadian Federal Income Tax Act* in reporting their federal income tax liabilities to The Canada Customs and Revenue Agency, formerly known as Revenue Canada, which is equivalent to the IRS in the United States. The federal tax calculation begins with an insurer's financial statements, prepared according to the *CICA Handbook*. As is true for insurers in the United States, insurers in Canada must consider the timing differences associated with amounts reported on the Canadian Annual Return and income tax returns.

One income tax that applies equally to insurance and non-insurance companies is the *business income tax*. But, as in the United States, to recognize the unique nature of long-term life insurance contracts, the business income tax requires certain special taxation provisions. For example, a significant factor in the income taxation of domestic life insurance companies and foreign non-life insurance companies is that Canadian taxable income is confined to that which is generated from the company's insurance business in Canada. This tax treatment contrasts with that of other Canadian businesses, including domestic non-life insurance companies, which pay income tax on their worldwide income and receive tax credits for any foreign income tax paid. Also, Canadian tax laws do not provide a tax deduction for small insurance companies.

Figure 8-6 summarizes the major components of gross income and tax deductions for insurers in the United States and Canada.

Premium Taxes

Premium taxes are taxes on an insurer's premium income earned within a state or province. The definition of premium income for tax purposes varies from state to state. Some states impose the tax on gross premiums, while other states allow companies to deduct the amount of policy dividends from the gross premium amount before calculating premium taxes. Some states require that the insurer pay the larger of the premium tax or the state income tax. State and provincial governments impose premium taxes on life insurance

FIGURE 8-6. Gross Income Components and Tax Deductions: United States and Canada.

UNITED STATES

Gross Income Components	Tax Deductions from Gross Income
Premium income on insurance and annuity products, including policy premiums, fees, deposits, and policy proceeds left with the insurer	Death benefits, other benefits, and insurance expenses
Investment income, including interest, dividends, and rental income	Increases in specified reserves
Capital gains, including increases in income resulting from the sale of stock, bond, and real estate investments	Policy dividends and experience rating refunds paid
Decreases in specified reserves, including contractual reserves, unearned premiums and unpaid losses on guaranteed renewable and noncancelable accident and health insurance policies, dividend accumulations for insurance and annuity products, and certain contingency reserves under group insurance contracts	Operating losses and capital losses
Other income, consisting of gross income that does not fall into any of the four categories above	Certain reinsurance considerations
	General corporate deductions for expenses
	Small life insurance company deduction

CANADA

Gross Income Components	Tax Deductions from Gross Income
Premium income, which consists of insurance premiums and annuity considerations from business in Canada	Contractual benefit costs
Gross investment income, which includes interest, taxable investment dividends, rents, and royalties	Interest paid by or credited to the insurer
Other income, which includes all other items of taxable income not included elsewhere, such as employee and employer contributions to pension and insurance funds for staff and agents, if these funds are held as a separate liability and not as part of contractual reserves	Expenses (excluding depreciation)
Realized and unrealized gains and losses on equities, which are included in income and are taxed at the usual corporate tax rate	Increase in actuarial reserves computed on a tax basis
The sale of specified debt obligations (SDOs), which creates a gain or loss that is amortized into income for both taxation and financial statement purposes	Dividends and experience rating refunds
	Capital cost allowances (CCAs), which are the amounts of depreciation expenses an insurer can deduct in calculating its taxable income

policies issued in that state or province. Taxation authorities calculate these taxes as a percentage of the premium income.

Fraternal benefit societies typically are exempt from premium taxes, although many states now impose premium taxes on specific non-profit insurance providers, such as Blue Cross/Blue Shield organizations. All Canadian provinces and some U.S. states do not impose taxes on annuity considerations. Annuity considerations typically are taxed at a lower rate than insurance premiums in those states that impose premium taxes on annuity considerations. Investment income and reinsurance premiums typically are excluded from the formula that determines the amount of premium taxes due from an insurer. Also, most states allow the insurer to deduct policyowner dividends from the amount of premium income used to calculate premium taxes due.

Accounting for premium taxes requires two basic sets of accounting entries: one to record taxes incurred and another to record the payment of the tax. Typically, when an insurer incurs premium taxes, the insurer makes the following accounting entry:

> **Premium Tax Expense.......xxx**
> **Premium Taxes Payable.................. xxx**
> To record incurred premium taxes.

Here, the insurer debits an expense account—*Premium Tax Expense*—and credits a liability account—*Premium Taxes Payable*—for the amount of premium taxes incurred. Upon payment of premium taxes, the insurer then makes a second accounting entry, as follows:

> **Premium Taxes Payable..........xxx**
> **Cash .... xxx**
> To record the payment of premium taxes.

Retaliatory Taxes

Nearly all states and some Canadian provinces have retaliatory tax laws, which are designed to protect domestic companies from unreasonable tax burdens placed upon them by other states or provinces. **Retaliatory tax laws** impose premium taxes on a *foreign insurer*, which is an insurer domiciled in another state, at the rate domestic companies in the state of domicile would be taxed by the foreign state, but only if the premium tax rate is higher in the state of domicile. Figure 8-7 shows an example of the effect of retaliatory tax laws on insurers.

Suppose State A has a premium tax rate of 1.5 percent and a retaliatory tax law and State B has a premium tax rate of 2 percent and no retaliatory tax law. In this example, insurers domiciled in State A would be subject to a premium tax rate of 1.5 percent on premiums written in State A. Moreover, because of the retaliatory tax law in State A, an insurer domiciled in State B that sells insurance in State A is subject to a 2 percent premium tax on business conducted in State A. If both states had the same premium tax rate, then the retaliatory tax law would not be needed and, thus, would not be imposed. Court decisions in the United States have tended to equalize the rates at which domestic and foreign insurers are taxed.

Guaranty-Fund Assessments—United States

Each state has established a guaranty association to protect policyowners in that state from losses as a result of insurer insolvency. In other words, if an insurance company becomes insolvent, the guaranty association covers the costs of providing benefits to the failed company's policyowners and beneficiaries. A guaranty association collects the money it needs to pay these benefits through **guaranty-fund assessments**, which are charges payable by sound insurers to the unsupported customer obligations of a failed insurer that had operated in a jurisdiction where sound insurers conduct business. Guaranty-fund assessments represent an expense for sound insurers. An insurance company that fails to pay a guaranty-fund assessment may have its insurance license revoked or suspended.

FIGURE 8-7. Retaliatory Premium Taxes.

Domiciled in ➔ Sells insurance in ⬇	State A (1.5%)	State B (2.0%)
State A (1.5%)	1.5%	2.0%
State B (2.0%)	2.0%	2.0%

CompCorp—Canada

The *Canadian Life and Health Insurance Compensation Corporation (CompCorp)* protects policyowners and beneficiaries throughout Canada. CompCorp operates similarly to state guaranty associations. The main difference is in coverage limits, which are beyond the scope of our discussion. For special circumstances, CompCorp may also borrow money from member companies. Insurers in Canada are required to be members of CompCorp and to make payments when requested. However, insurers in Canada cannot offset these payments against premium taxes, as insurers in the United States can do with guaranty-fund assessments.

Key Terms and Concepts

investment expenses
general and administrative
   expenses
operating expenses
acquisition expenses
development expenses
control account
reinsurance commissions
maintenance expenses
overhead expenses

life insurance company taxable
   income (LICTI)
tentative LICTI
premium taxes
retaliatory tax laws
guaranty-fund assessments
Canadian Life and Health
   Insurance Compensation
   Corporation (CompCorp)

Chapter 9

Financial Ratio Analysis of Life Insurance Companies

OBJECTIVES

After reading this chapter, you should be able to

⊕ Identify the numerator and denominator of a financial ratio

⊕ Recognize how changes in the numerator or denominator of a financial ratio will affect the value of the ratio

⊕ Compare horizontal analysis with vertical analysis

⊕ Calculate the result of a financial ratio using given values for the numerator and denominator

⊕ Distinguish among common financial ratios that fall into each of these categories: liquidity, activity, leverage, capital and surplus, and profitability

*F*inancial ratio analysis is an important diagnostic tool for both internal and external customers of an insurance company. ***Financial ratio analysis*** consists of calculating the relationships between various pairs of financial statement values for the purpose of assessing a company's financial condition or performance. The financial statements that analysts study most often are the balance sheet, the income statement, and the cash flow statement. Financial ratio analysis serves to point out changes or trends in operating performance.

In addition, financial ratio analysis helps to highlight a company's strengths and weaknesses in its environment. For example, acceptable financial ratio results for a clothing manufacturer most likely will differ from those of an insurance company. Also, financial ratio analysis can answer yes/no questions, such as whether short-term debts can be paid on time and whether the company is efficiently using its assets to generate profits. This chapter discusses financial ratio analysis as it applies to insurers in the United States and Canada. We also discuss some commonly used financial ratios and indicate the type of information typically provided by these ratios. Keep in mind that you may find a slightly different calculation for the same ratio in another textbook or in your own company.

A ***financial ratio*** is a percentage amount that expresses a relationship between two pieces of financial information. When a financial ratio is expressed in fraction form, the number on the top part of the fraction is the *numerator* and the number in the bottom part of the fraction is the *denominator*. Figure 9-1 summarizes the rules for interpreting changes in financial ratios.

FIGURE 9-1. Rules for Interpreting Changes in Financial Ratios.

The value of a financial ratio will *increase* if the value of the

- Numerator increases while the value of the denominator remains unchanged
- Denominator decreases while the value of the numerator remains unchanged

The value of a financial ratio will *decrease* if the value of the

- Numerator decreases while the value of the denominator remains unchanged
- Denominator increases while the value of the numerator remains unchanged

Recall that many insurance companies in the United States prepare financial statements under two primary accounting bases: U.S. GAAP and statutory accounting. Generally, financial analysts prefer to use GAAP-based financial statements when they analyze an insurer's profitability and statutory-based financial statements when they analyze insurer solvency. However, they can analyze whatever data they have available. Also recall that, in Canada, GAAP-based financial statements are used for analyzing both solvency and profitability.

Before we discuss specific financial ratios of interest to insurers, we first discuss briefly comparative financial statement analysis.

Comparative Analysis

Both internal and external customers of a company conduct financial ratio analysis. **Internal analysis** is financial ratio analysis undertaken by employees of the company being analyzed. An insurance company's management uses financial ratios to measure performance at all levels of the company. **External analysis** is financial ratio analysis performed by someone outside of the company being analyzed. Customers of an insurer, as well as independent rating agencies, conduct financial ratio analysis to evaluate the claims-paying ability of the insurer. Insurance company stockholders and other investors conduct financial ratio analysis to evaluate the company's overall profitability. Insurance company regulators use financial ratio analysis to evaluate an insurer's solvency.

A company's financial statements from a specified accounting period do not tell a complete story. However, by comparing two sets of numbers that reflect company operations during the same accounting period or by analyzing the change in an item over a period of time, you can gain insight into the company's financial condition and performance. **Comparative financial statements** present data for two or more accounting periods. Comparative financial statements can present the year-to-year changes in terms of absolute numerical amounts and percentages or ratios.

Two common types of comparative analysis are horizontal analysis and vertical analysis. **Horizontal analysis** is a type of financial statement analysis that involves calculating the absolute amount and the percentage of the increase or decrease in a specified financial statement from one reporting period to another. The earliest financial reporting period used in horizontal analysis is known as the **base period**. To calculate the absolute amount of the change, subtract the base period amount from that of the period under study, then divide the difference by the base period amount, as follows:

$$\text{Absolute amount} = \frac{\text{(Period under study amount} - \text{Base period amount)}}{\text{(Base period amount)}}$$

To calculate the percentage change, we multiply the absolute amount by 100, as follows:

$$\text{Percentage} = \frac{\text{(Period under study amount} - \text{Base period amount)} \times 100}{\text{(Base period amount)}}$$

Trend analysis, also called *trend percentages* or *index-number trend analysis,* is a specific type of horizontal analysis that involves calculating percentage changes in financial statement figures over several successive accounting periods, rather than over just two periods. A **trend** is a change that occurs over time. Comparative financial statements indicate the direction and velocity of trends. *Direction* refers to whether a trend displays an increase or decrease in an account. *Velocity* refers to whether the increase or decrease in an account is gradual or rapid.

To conduct trend analysis, use the following procedure:

1. Select a base period and assign it an index number of 100 percent. An **index number** is a number that provides a statistical method for measuring the change in a variable.

2. Calculate a series of index numbers for the other periods in relation to the base period.

Use the following rules to interpret index numbers:

- An index number greater than 100 indicates an increase in a variable from the base period. For example, an index number of 120 indicates a 20 percent increase from the base period.

- An index number less than 100 indicates a decrease in the variable from the base period. For example, an index number of 80 indicates a 20 percent decrease from the base period.

Vertical analysis is a type of financial statement analysis that reveals the relationship of each financial statement item to a specified financial statement item during the same reporting period. To conduct vertical analysis of the balance sheet and the income statement, a company would divide each:

Balance Sheet	Income Statement
Asset account by total assets	Revenue account by total revenues
Liabilities and Owners' Equity account by total liabilities and owners' equity	Expense account by total expenses

We can also use vertical analysis to compile a ***common-size financial statement***, which is a financial statement that consists of the percentages obtained from vertical analysis. Common-size financial statements display only percentages, not monetary amounts. The balance sheet and the income statement are often exhibited as common-size statements. Each line item on a common-sized balance sheet is expressed as a percentage of (1) total assets or (2) total liabilities plus owners' equity. In other words, total assets is the "common size" to which we relate the balance sheet's other asset amounts. Total liabilities and owners' equity is the "common size" to which we relate the balance sheet's liabilities and owners' equity.

Because amounts on common-size financial statements are stated in relative terms rather than in absolute terms, the use of common-size statements facilitates comparison of companies of different sizes in the same industry. It also facilitates somewhat the comparison of companies in different industries. Suppose Company A's net income is three times that of Company B. You might assume that Company A is the more profitable company. However, by examining common-size income statements for both companies, you might discover that Company B's net income represents a greater percentage of its total revenues than that of Company A. Thus, although Company B's net income is lower, we can deduce from this one comparison that Company B appears to be operating more efficiently than Company A.

Types of Financial Ratios

For illustrative purposes, whenever possible throughout this chapter, we will conduct financial ratio analysis on the Grand Life Insurance Company's balance sheet and income statement, which are shown in Figures 9-2 and 9-3.

Key financial ratios measure an insurer's (1) liquidity, (2) activity, (3) leverage, (4) capital and surplus, and (5) profitability. Figure 9-4

FIGURE 9-2. Balance Sheet: Grand Life Insurance Company.

Grand File Insurance Company
Balance Sheet
as of December 31, 2001

Assets

Securities available for sale	
Debt securities	12,204,000
Equity securities	500,380
Total securities available for sale	12,704,380
Policy loans	1,392,580
Cash and cash equivalents	634,696
Property and equipment	93,404
Total assets	14,825,060

Liabilities and Owners' Equity

Liabilities:	
Contractual liabilities:	
Future contractual benefits:	
Life	7,018,245
Health	3,315,422
Unpaid claims	122,894
Total Contractual liabilities	10,456,561
Other Liabilities:	
Accounts payable	193,732
Amounts due to reinsurers	124,730
Dividends payable to stockholders	272,511
Long-term liabilities	123,558
Total liabilities	11,171,092
Owners' Equity:	
Common stock, $0.02 par value; 6,000,000	
shares authorized; 1,000,000 outstanding	20,000
Additional paid-in capital	641,356
Unrealized capital gain (loss), net	112,230
Retained earnings	2,880,382
Total owners' equity	3,653,968
Total liabilities and owners' equity	14,825,060

depicts generic ratios of liquidity, activity, leverage, capital, and profitability.

FIGURE 9-3. Income Statement: Grand Life Insurance Company.

Grand Life Insurance Company
Income Statement
for the year ended December 31, 2001

Revenues

Premiums:	
Life	3,656,220
Health	1,509,458
Net investment income	1,758,592
Other	24,906
Total revenues	6,949,176

Expenses

Contractual benefits:	
Death benefits and other contractual benefits	2,151,479
Health benefits	1,055,632
Increase in liability for future contractual benefits	55,402
Total contractual benefits	3,262,513
Expenses:	
Commissions and fees	189,074
Salaries	922,811
Other operating expenses	1,392,314
Total expenses	2,504,199
Total benefits and expenses	5,766,712
Earnings before interest and taxes	1,182,464
Interest expense	7,413
Earnings before income taxes	1,175,051
Income tax expense (40%)	470,020
Net Income	705,031
Earnings per share of common stock:	
Net earnings per share	0.71

Because the financial ratios in Figure 9-4 are generic, they are not necessarily applicable to the insurance industry. Many of these generic ratios have been modified for analyzing insurance companies. The following sections describe the most common financial ratios that analysts use to study an insurer's liquidity, activity, leverage, capital, and profitability.

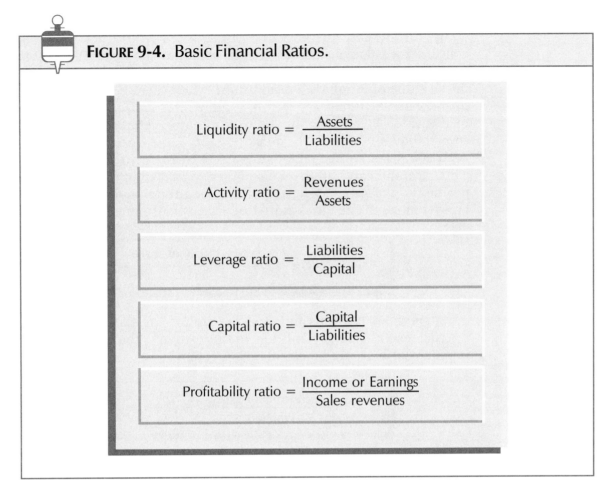

FIGURE 9-4. Basic Financial Ratios.

$$\text{Liquidity ratio} = \frac{\text{Assets}}{\text{Liabilities}}$$

$$\text{Activity ratio} = \frac{\text{Revenues}}{\text{Assets}}$$

$$\text{Leverage ratio} = \frac{\text{Liabilities}}{\text{Capital}}$$

$$\text{Capital ratio} = \frac{\text{Capital}}{\text{Liabilities}}$$

$$\text{Profitability ratio} = \frac{\text{Income or Earnings}}{\text{Sales revenues}}$$

Liquidity Ratios

Recall from Chapter 2 that *liquidity* is the ease with which an asset can be converted into cash for an approximation of its true value. **Liquidity ratios** measure a company's ability to meet its maturing short-term obligations. Recall from earlier discussions that short-term obligations are expected to come due within one year. For insurers, *illiquidity*—that is, the lack of liquidity—is a commonly used predictor of potential trouble because insurers must have enough cash and other liquid assets when needed to pay contractual benefits and general business expenses.

However, highly liquid assets produce little or no return. Thus, excessive liquidity damages profits. Consequently, the goal for insurance companies is to maintain a moderate level of liquidity. For insurance companies, liquidity ratios generally contain liquid assets in the numerator and reserves in the denominator, as follows:

$$\frac{\text{Liquid assets}}{\text{Reserves}}$$

Liquid assets include cash and readily marketable assets. Generally, an increase in the value of a liquidity ratio between two consecutive balance sheet dates indicates that the insurer has more liquidity now than during the previous reporting period. An increase in the value of a liquidity ratio results when there is (1) an increase in the value of liquid assets in the numerator and/or (2) a decrease in the value of reserves in the denominator. A critical insurance-specific liquidity ratio is the quick liquidity ratio. The *quick liquidity ratio* compares an insurer's liquid assets to its contractual reserves. This ratio indicates an insurer's ability to make contractual benefit payments without having to sell its long-term invested assets or borrow money. The quick liquidity ratio is calculated as follows:

$$\text{Quick liquidity ration} = \frac{\text{Liquid assets}}{\text{Contractual reserves}}$$

Suppose an insurer's liquid assets are $0.5 million and its contractual reserves are $2.5 million. In this example, the insurer's quick liquidity ratio would be calculated as follows:

$$\frac{\$0.5 \text{ million}}{\$2.5 \text{ million}} = 0.2 = 20 \text{ percent}$$

Activity Ratios

Activity ratios, also called *operating efficiency ratios* or *turnover ratios*, measure the speed with which various assets are converted into sales or cash. Activity ratios thus gauge the productivity and efficiency of a company. There are several versions of the asset turnover ratio. Each requires dividing a company's total revenues by the company's assets, such as cash, invested assets, or fixed assets. An important asset turnover ratio for insurance companies is *total asset turnover,* which measures how efficiently a company has used its total assets to generate revenues, as follows:

$$\text{Total asset turnover} = \frac{\text{Total revenues}}{\text{Total assets}}$$

In the numerator, we use total revenues because, for an insurer, generating investment income and fee income is usually part of the insurer's core business operations. Also, we use the amount of total assets at the end of the reporting period in the denominator. Generally, the higher a firm's total asset turnover, the more efficiently it has used its assets. Suppose the total asset turnover for Company A is 1.0 and the total asset turnover for Company B is 2.0. In other words, Company B has generated $2 for each $1 invested in total assets, while Company A has generated only $1 for each $1 invested in total assets. Thus, we could infer that Company B has used its assets more efficiently.

Grand's total asset turnover is calculated as follows:

$$\frac{\$6,949,176}{\$14,825,060} = 0.47$$

This information indicates that Grand generated $0.47 for every $1 invested in total assets.

Leverage Ratios

The leverage effect is an important concept in finance. The **leverage effect**, also called *leverage*, can be defined as a financial effect in which the presence of fixed costs—either operating costs or financing costs—automatically magnifies the potential risks and returns to the company's owners. As a company's leverage increases, the company's exposure to risk of loss increases. Thus, the company's potential for earnings also increases. Conversely, as a company's leverage decreases, the company's risk of loss decreases, so the company's earnings potential also decreases.

Leverage ratios are financial ratios used to compare the amount of an insurer's obligations with the insurer's ability to meet those obligations. For insurance-specific leverage ratios, liabilities can be defined as (1) contractual reserves or (2) contractual reserves plus other types of reserves and/or other liabilities. Generally, the lower the value of the leverage ratio, the stronger the insurer's financial position. A decrease in the value of a leverage ratio results from (1) a decrease in the value of liabilities in the numerator and/or (2) an increase in the value of capital and surplus in the denominator. We describe several insurance-specific leverage ratios after we describe the types of leverage.

Types of Leverage

The leverage effect applies to all companies, including insurance companies. Three main types of leverage are (1) operating leverage, (2) financial leverage, and (3) total leverage. **Operating leverage** is the effect whereby incurring fixed operating costs automatically magnifies a company's risks and potential returns. **Financial leverage** is the effect whereby incurring fixed financing costs—usually borrowed funds—automatically magnifies a company's risks and potential returns. **Total leverage**—the combined effect of operating leverage and financial leverage—represents the effect whereby incurring these fixed costs automatically magnifies both risks and potential returns to a company's owners.

Positive Leverage and Negative Leverage

Operating leverage, financial leverage, and total leverage can be either positive or negative. The effect of earning a larger profit as a result of leverage is called a **positive leverage effect**. The effect of earning a lower profit because of the presence of leverage is called a **negative leverage effect**. For example, if the assets in which a company's borrowed funds are invested earn a rate of return greater than the fixed rate of return required by the suppliers of borrowed funds, the result is *positive financial leverage*. This positive difference boosts overall returns for the company's owners. On the other hand, suppose the company incurs additional fixed operating costs, but then fails to earn enough operating profits to cover these added costs. In this case, the company experiences *negative operating leverage* because the company will have lower profits than if it had not incurred the additional fixed operating costs.

If a company borrows funds, invests the funds, and earns a return greater than the interest expense the company must pay to the lender, then the company earns a return that it would not otherwise have earned. The difference between the cost of borrowing the funds and the return earned using these funds is called the **margin**, or the *spread*, *marginal return*, or *profit margin*. Suppose a company can borrow money at 9 percent interest. If the company earns an 11 percent return on those borrowed funds, the company has realized positive financial leverage with a margin of 2 percent. However, the company has incurred a fixed financing cost—interest expense—and this financial leverage has magnified both risk and potential return. Moreover, if the company is unable to earn at least 9 percent on the borrowed funds, the company will lose money. Thus, the company would be in a worse financial position than if it had not borrowed the funds.

Debt-to-Surplus Ratio

For non-insurance stock companies, a key leverage ratio is the debt-to-equity ratio, which measures the relationship between the company's liabilities and its owners' equity. For insurance companies, especially mutual and fraternal insurers, a key leverage ratio is the debt-to-surplus ratio. The **debt-to-surplus ratio** is calculated by dividing total liabilities by total surplus, as follows:

$$\text{Debt-to-surplus ratio} = \frac{\text{Total liabilities}}{\text{Surplus}}$$

The higher an insurer's debt-to-surplus ratio, the more the insurer relies on borrowed funds to pay for current and future contractual obligations, to pay for ongoing business operations, and to finance growth. Insurers therefore aim to have a low debt-to-surplus ratio, all other factors remaining equal.

Suppose Grand has $11,000,000 in total liabilities and $2,000,000 in surplus. Grand's debt-to-surplus ratio is calculated as follows:

$$\frac{\$11,000,000}{\$2,000,000} = 5.5$$

Insurance Leverage Ratio

The **insurance leverage ratio**, also called the *gross leverage ratio*, is the ratio of contractual reserves to capital and surplus. This ratio focuses on an insurer's contractual obligations and is calculated as follows:

$$\text{Insurance leverage ratio} = \frac{\text{Contractual reserves}}{\text{Capital and surplus}}$$

A low result for the insurance leverage ratio is generally more desirable than a high result.

Surplus Relief Ratio

Recall that surplus relief generally refers to the improvement of an insurer's capital and surplus position from the use of reinsurance. Ceding risk to a reinsurer can be viewed as an alternative source of financing for insurers, thus producing a leverage effect. The surplus relief ratio measures an insurer's use of reinsurance—as the ceding company and the reinsurer. The **surplus relief ratio** compares the insurer's net cost for ceding reinsurance or net earnings from assuming reinsurance to the insurer's capital and surplus, as follows:

$$\text{Surplus relief ratio} = \frac{\text{Net cost for or net income from reinsurance}}{\text{Capital and surplus}}$$

A positive value for the surplus relief ratio usually indicates that the insurer ceded more reinsurance coverage than it assumed. A very large positive value for the surplus relief ratio may indicate that the insurer has obtained large amounts of reinsurance in order to increase its capital and surplus. A negative value for the surplus relief ratio usually indicates that the insurer assumed more reinsurance than it ceded. A very large negative value for the surplus relief ratio might indicate that the insurer is straining its capital and surplus.

Figure 9-5 summarizes the common leverage ratios used by life insurance companies.

Capital and Surplus Ratios

Insurance companies measure their financial strength using capital and surplus ratios. **Capital and surplus ratios**, also called *capitalization ratios*—and sometimes referred to as simply *capital ratios* for stock companies and *surplus ratios* for mutual companies—are financial ratios used to express the relationship between an insurer's capital and surplus and its liabilities. The general forms of the capital and surplus ratios for insurers as follows:

$$\text{Capital and surplus ratio} = \frac{\text{Capital and surplus}}{\text{Total liabilities}}$$

$$\text{Capital ratio} = \frac{\text{Capital}}{\text{Total liabilities}}$$

$$\text{Surplus ratio} = \frac{\text{Surplus}}{\text{Total liabilities}}$$

Suppose Grand's capital equals $600,000 and total liabilities equals $11,000,000. Grand's capital ratio is calculated as follows:

$$\frac{\$600,000}{\$11,000,000} = 0.545 = 5.5\%$$

Generally, the greater the value of capital and surplus ratios, the stronger the insurer's financial position. A drawback of the basic capital and surplus ratio is that it is based on unweighted values, which result in unweighted ratios. Unweighted capital and surplus ratios are not suitable for comparing different insurers that have different exposures to risk. To account for different risk levels, financial analysts typically apply weighted values. A **weighted value** is an

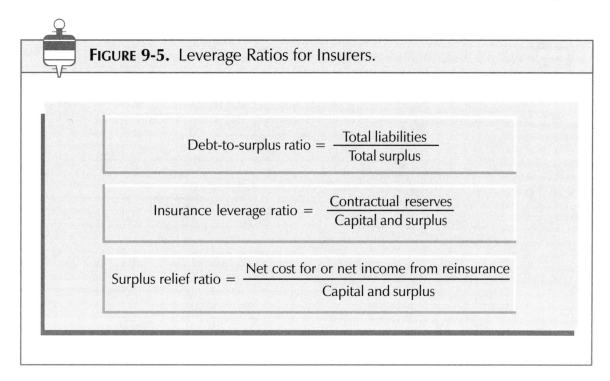

FIGURE 9-5. Leverage Ratios for Insurers.

$$\text{Debt-to-surplus ratio} = \frac{\text{Total liabilities}}{\text{Total surplus}}$$

$$\text{Insurance leverage ratio} = \frac{\text{Contractual reserves}}{\text{Capital and surplus}}$$

$$\text{Surplus relief ratio} = \frac{\text{Net cost for or net income from reinsurance}}{\text{Capital and surplus}}$$

amount that has been multiplied by a percentage. Some common reasons for weighting a value are to indicate the (1) effect that risk has on the value, (2) age of a particular value, or (3) share of a total amount that the value represents.

To obtain a more accurate measure of an insurer's financial strength, insurers, regulators, and rating agencies use capital and surplus ratios that are weight-adjusted to account for different levels of capital risk and different reserving practices that are unique to each insurer. Ratios that use weighted values are called *weighted ratios*. These specialized capital and surplus ratios are known as the NAIC's *risk-based capital requirements* in the United States and the *Minimum Continuing Capital and Surplus Requirements* in Canada. We discuss these specific weighted capital and surplus ratios in Chapter 10 in the context of regulatory monitoring of insurance company solvency.

Profitability Ratios

Profitability ratios measure the success of a company's growth and focus on whether the company is prospering. An increase in the value of a profitability ratio generally indicates greater profitability. Figure 9-6 summarizes profitability ratios that are commonly used for analyzing the GAAP-based financial statements of non-insurance companies.

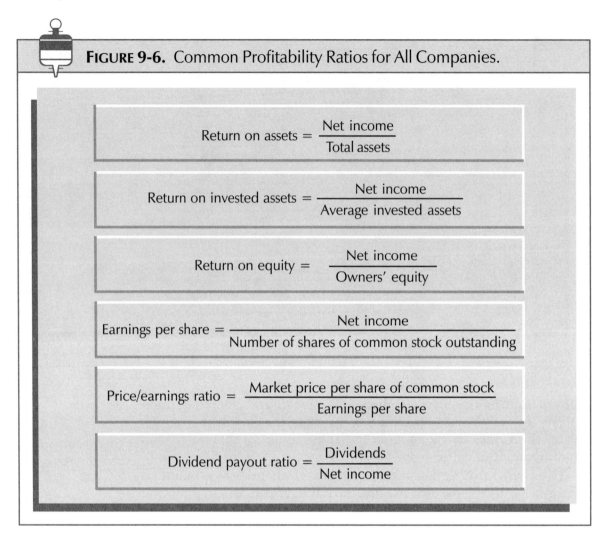

FIGURE 9-6. Common Profitability Ratios for All Companies.

$$\text{Return on assets} = \frac{\text{Net income}}{\text{Total assets}}$$

$$\text{Return on invested assets} = \frac{\text{Net income}}{\text{Average invested assets}}$$

$$\text{Return on equity} = \frac{\text{Net income}}{\text{Owners' equity}}$$

$$\text{Earnings per share} = \frac{\text{Net income}}{\text{Number of shares of common stock outstanding}}$$

$$\text{Price/earnings ratio} = \frac{\text{Market price per share of common stock}}{\text{Earnings per share}}$$

$$\text{Dividend payout ratio} = \frac{\text{Dividends}}{\text{Net income}}$$

Profitability ratios for insurers typically compare a gain from operations in the numerator to the resources employed or invested to earn the gain. Generally, an increase in the value of a profitability ratio indicates higher profitability. An increase in the value of a profitability ratio results from (1) an increase in the value of the gain from operations in the numerator and/or (2) a decrease in the value of the assets invested or equity used in the denominator. In choosing an appropriate measure of profit, you could choose an insurer's profits before taxes or profits after taxes. The following sections describe key profitability ratios for insurance companies.

Return on Capital Ratio

The *return on capital ratio* is the percentage return an insurer has earned on its capital and surplus. This ratio is calculated by dividing earnings by total capital employed. The result of the return on capital ratio indicates how efficiently an insurer's managers are employing capital and surplus to earn a return for the insurer's owners. The return on capital ratio is similar to the traditional return on equity (ROE) ratio depicted in Figure 9-4. Whereas ROE is stated as the ratio of net income to owners' equity, the return on capital ratio is typically expressed as the ratio of net gain from operations to beginning capital and surplus, as follows:

$$\text{Return on capital ratio} = \frac{\text{Net gain from operations}}{\text{Beginning capital and surplus}}$$

Suppose Grand's net gain from operations equals $1,000,000 and its beginning capital and surplus equals $600,000. Grand's return on capital ratio is calculated as follows:

$$\frac{\$1,000,000}{\$600,000} = 1.67$$

Gross Profit Ratio

The gross profit ratio provides a simple measure of the growth of an insurer's capital and surplus. The **gross profit ratio**, developed by the A.M. Best Company, compares an insurer's contributions to capital during a reporting period to its beginning capital and surplus for the period. This ratio is expressed as follows:

$$\text{Gross profit ratio} = \frac{\text{Gross contributions to capital and surplus}}{\text{Beginning capital and surplus}}$$

Net Gain to Total Income Ratio

Insurers use the **net gain to total income ratio** to measure the share of operating income—operating income minus operating expenses—that represents the insurer's net profit. In this context, net gain means *net gain from operations*, which is the net gain before subtracting dividends and federal income taxes. This ratio highlights the share of the insurer's income that is not used to cover expenses. The net gain to total income ratio is calculated as follows:

$$\text{Net gain to total income ratio} = \frac{\text{Net gain from operations}}{\text{Total income} + \text{Realized capital gains and losses}}$$

Investment Yield Ratio

The **investment yield ratio**, also called the *net yield*, shows how efficiently the insurer used its invested assets to earn a return. This ratio compares the insurer's investment income to the insurer's average invested assets for the reporting period, as follows:

$$\text{Investment yield ratio} = \frac{\text{Investment income}}{\text{Average invested assets}}$$

An unusually high investment yield could indicate excessively risky investments, whereas a low investment yield usually indicates inadequate returns on invested assets. Thus, an insurer's investment managers seek an investment yield that is neither too high nor too low, although a definition of these extremes varies by insurance company.

Figure 9-7 summarizes key insurance-specific profitability ratios.

Figure 9-8 summarizes the key financial ratios discussed in this chapter.

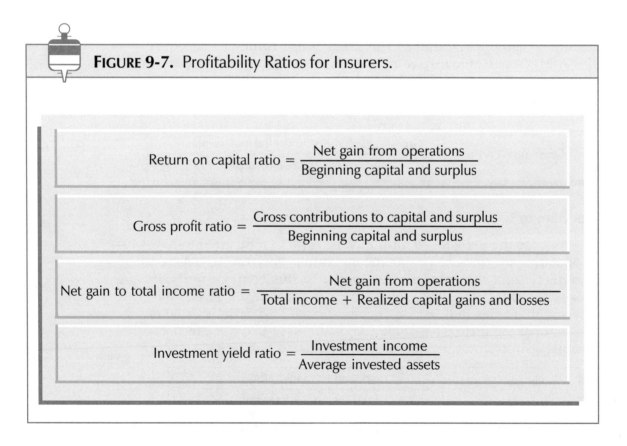

FIGURE 9-7. Profitability Ratios for Insurers.

$$\text{Return on capital ratio} = \frac{\text{Net gain from operations}}{\text{Beginning capital and surplus}}$$

$$\text{Gross profit ratio} = \frac{\text{Gross contributions to capital and surplus}}{\text{Beginning capital and surplus}}$$

$$\text{Net gain to total income ratio} = \frac{\text{Net gain from operations}}{\text{Total income} + \text{Realized capital gains and losses}}$$

$$\text{Investment yield ratio} = \frac{\text{Investment income}}{\text{Average invested assets}}$$

FIGURE 9-8. Key Financial Ratios for Insurers.

LIQUIDITY RATIO

$$\text{Quick liquidity ratio} = \frac{\text{Liquid assets}}{\text{Contractual reserves}}$$

ACTIVITY RATIO

$$\text{Total asset turnover} = \frac{\text{Total revenues}}{\text{Total assets}}$$

LEVERAGE RATIOS

$$\text{Debt-to-surplus ratio} = \frac{\text{Total liabilities}}{\text{Total surplus}}$$

$$\text{Insurance leverage ratio} = \frac{\text{Contractual reserves}}{\text{Capital and surplus}}$$

$$\text{Surplus relief ratio} = \frac{\text{Net cost for or net income from reinsurance}}{\text{Capital and surplus}}$$

CAPITAL AND SURPLUS RATIOS

$$\text{Capital and surplus ratio} = \frac{\text{Capital and surplus}}{\text{Total liabilities}}$$

$$\text{Capital ratio} = \frac{\text{Capital}}{\text{Total liabilities}}$$

$$\text{Surplus ratio} = \frac{\text{Surplus}}{\text{Total liabilities}}$$

PROFITABILITY RATIOS

$$\text{Return on capital ratio} = \frac{\text{Net gain from operations}}{\text{Beginning capital and surplus}}$$

$$\text{Gross profit ratio} = \frac{\text{Gross contributions to capital and surplus}}{\text{Beginning capital and surplus}}$$

$$\text{Net gain to total income ratio} = \frac{\text{Net gain from operations}}{\text{Total income + Realized capital gains and losses}}$$

$$\text{Investment yield ratio} = \frac{\text{Investment income}}{\text{Average invested assets}}$$

Key Terms and Concepts

financial ratio analysis
financial ratio
internal analysis
external analysis
comparative financial
   statements
horizontal analysis
base period
trend analysis
trend
index number
vertical analysis
common-size financial
   statement
liquidity ratios
liquid assets
quick liquidity ratio
activity ratios
total asset turnover

leverage effect
leverage ratios
operating leverage
financial leverage
total leverage
positive leverage effect
negative leverage effect
margin
debt-to-surplus ratio
insurance leverage ratio
surplus relief ratio
capital and surplus ratios
weighted value
profitability ratios
return on capital ratio
gross profit ratio
net gain to total income ratio
investment yield ratio

Chapter 10

Regulatory Monitoring of Life Insurance Companies

OBJECTIVES

After reading this chapter, you should be able to

◉ Recognize the function of IRIS ratios, the FAST system, scenario analysis, and onsite regulatory examinations with respect to insurer solvency in the United States

◉ Recognize and distinguish among risk-based capital requirements (United States) and Minimum Continuing Capital and Surplus Requirements (Canada) in monitoring insurance company solvency

◉ Recognize the function of scenario analysis and onsite regulatory examinations with respect to insurer solvency in Canada

I n Chapter 9, we discussed financial ratio analysis of a life insurer's financial statements. Chapter 10 discusses regulatory monitoring of insurance company solvency in the United States and Canada. Government regulators, who have the primary responsibility for monitoring solvency, use financial ratio analysis and other tools to routinely measure and monitor insurer solvency. The specific tools used to measure and monitor solvency differ between the United States and Canada, as shown in the following sections.

Regulatory Monitoring in the United States

State insurance regulators—with assistance and guidance from the National Association of Insurance Commissioners (NAIC)—routinely monitor the financial condition of insurers in order to prevent insurer insolvency. The U.S. Annual Statement is the primary basis for solvency monitoring by government regulators in the United States. Recall that the Annual Statement is a financial report, prepared using statutory accounting practices, that every insurer in the United States must file annually and quarterly with the NAIC and in every state in which the insurer conducts business. The U.S. Annual Statement is commonly referred to as the *U.S. Statutory Statement* because insurers are required to file this statement on a quarterly basis. The U.S. Annual Statement includes a balance sheet (Assets page and a Liabilities and Surplus page), an income statement (Summary of Operations page), cash flow statement, notes to the financial statements, and various schedules and exhibits.

Most of the financial information in these Annual Statement filings is stored in the NAIC's financial database, which state insurance departments can access electronically. Insurance company financial statements come under intense scrutiny from government regulators. This scrutiny is intended to identify potential solvency problems so regulators can initiate preventive measures to avert insurer insolvency. To aid them in this task, regulators use several tools and measures developed specifically for the purpose of analyzing the financial statements of insurance companies. Common regulatory measures of financial statement analysis that apply to most insurers operating in the United States include

- Insurance Regulatory Information System (IRIS) ratios

- The Financial Analysis and Solvency Tracking (FAST) system

- Scenario analysis

- Risk-based capital requirements

- Onsite regulatory examinations

Insurance Regulatory Information System Ratios

Insurance regulators in the United States use a set of specific financial ratios, called the **Insurance Regulatory Information System (IRIS) ratios**, to monitor life insurance companies. The NAIC and the A.M. Best Company developed this system. State insurance departments use the twelve IRIS ratios to identify insurance companies that are most likely to experience financial difficulty. The first eight ratios are tests of an insurance company's solvency and profitability. The remaining four IRIS ratios are tests of a company's financial stability.

The IRIS ratios identify wide swings in operational results, such as changes in premium income or contractual reserves. If an insurer's IRIS ratio results do not fall within the normal range, regulators may raise questions about the insurer's ability to manage its operations. Insurers often calculate and monitor their IRIS ratios so the insurer's management can take corrective measures before an unfavorable review by insurance regulators becomes necessary. Insurers that conduct business in the United States submit to the IRIS tests. IRIS consists of two phases, which are described in Figure 10-1.

FIGURE 10-1. Phases of IRIS.

STATISTICAL PHASE	The statistical phase uses the 12 standardized financial IRIS ratios to identify companies that show results outside a *usual* (normal) range. A result outside the usual range is called an *exception*. The NAIC calculates the IRIS ratios using statutory data extracted from the U.S. Annual Statement, then provides the results of these tests in a report to state insurance departments and to the insurance company. This report includes the IRIS ratio results for the company and the percentile rankings of all life insurance companies.
ANALYTICAL PHASE	In the analytical phase, a team of financial examiners analyzes the U.S. Annual Statement and IRIS ratio results of specified insurance companies. This phase is generally reserved for insurance companies whose statistical phase revealed four or more ratios outside the usual range.

Financial Analysis and Solvency Tracking System

Large insurance companies are subject to a solvency analysis known as the Financial Analysis and Solvency Tracking System. The *Financial Analysis and Solvency Tracking (FAST) system* uses two types of analysis to examine large insurers' financial statement information: (1) ratio analysis of the insurer's most recent financial statements and (2) analysis of the five-year history of specific aspects of the insurer's financial statements. The NAIC chooses the aspects for analysis on a case-by-case basis.

If regulators find unusual results during the FAST analysis, the NAIC contacts the insurer's state of domicile for further information about the insurer's financial condition and to learn any new regulatory action the state has taken against the insurer. If the NAIC determines that the state has taken appropriate action toward the insurer, then the NAIC may either end its involvement in the case or continue to monitor the insurer. If the NAIC finds that the state's regulatory action toward the insurer is inadequate, then the NAIC will recommend further action. If the state does not follow the NAIC's recommendation, then the NAIC notifies the other states in which the insurer does business and coordinates all the states' actions toward the insurer.

Scenario Analysis

Most insurers in the United States are required to apply a limited form of scenario analysis annually on interest-sensitive products such as variable life insurance and variable annuities. *Scenario analysis*, a technique that employs quantitative modeling, involves entering different sets of data into a model and then determining how changes in the input data affect the model's output. The following sections describe two common types of scenario analysis.

Cash-Flow Testing

One type of scenario analysis commonly used for valuing an insurer's liabilities whose cash flows are sensitive to interest rates is cash-flow testing. *Cash-flow testing (CFT)* is the process of projecting the cash flows associated with an insurer's existing business and comparing the timing and amounts of cash flows for assets and liabilities after the valuation date. Cash-flow testing is performed using scenarios of assumed future economic and operating conditions.

Dynamic Financial Analysis

Dynamic financial analysis (DFA) is a form of scenario analysis, broader in scope than cash-flow testing, in which insurers use simulation modeling and multiple-scenario testing to project future values for an insurer's assets, liabilities, and owners' equity. Although U.S. insurance regulators do not require its use, DFA is of particular importance in developing an insurer's decision-support information for a single product. By testing a large number of randomly generated, user-defined assumptions over a series of multiple iterations of a given product, DFA helps to identify a likely range of values for various aspects of a product's future experience, given a set of product management strategies. DFA helps an insurer to identify scenarios that may pose financial problems, as well as identify actions that the insurer can take to resolve problematic scenarios.

Risk-Based Capital Requirements

Insurers operate under different levels of risk. For example, one insurer might invest heavily in low-risk bonds, whereas another insurer may invest heavily in high-risk bonds. The difference in financial strength is not apparent from calculating the capital and surplus ratio for each insurer, because the capital and surplus ratio does not consider the different levels of risks associated with invested assets. Thus, both insurers might have the same capital and surplus ratio results, but the insurer that invests in the high-risk bonds is following a riskier investment strategy. Consequently, this insurer may not be as financially strong as is the insurer that follows a more conservative investment strategy.

The NAIC drafted risk-based capital requirements, which use weighted values, to help regulators monitor insurance company financial strength and solvency. The NAIC's **risk-based capital (RBC) requirements** determine the minimum capital level of an insurer of that insurer's size and risk profile, as identified by a specific RBC formula. The RBC formula requires that an insurer's total risk be evaluated relative to four classifications of risk, called **C risks,** or *contingency risks*, that are intrinsic to an insurer's invested assets and the products that it underwrites. Figure 10-2 describes these C risks.

The calculation of the NAIC's RBC formula is beyond the scope of this textbook. Regulators compare RBC ratios with trigger points to determine if regulatory intervention is necessary, and, if so, to what degree. Because risk-based capital is the minimum threshold capital required, insurance companies aim to have a significantly higher amount of capital and surplus—in effect, a safety cushion—than is otherwise required using the RBC formula.

Onsite Regulatory Examinations

Another tool that insurance regulators use to monitor the solvency of insurers is the routine **onsite regulatory examination.** Onsite regulatory examinations usually consist of two parts:

FIGURE 10-2. Risk-Based Capital: C Risks.

C-1 risk (asset risk)	The risk that the insurer will lose asset value on its investments such as stocks, bonds, mortgages, and real estate. Examples of C-1 risk include the loss in market value of assets (except if caused by interest-rate movements, which is a C-3 risk) and a borrower's failure to pay principal and/or interest owed to the insurer.
C-2 risk (pricing risk)	The risk that the insurer's experience with mortality or expenses will differ significantly from expectations, causing the insurer to lose money on its products. Examples of C-2 risk include a decrease in life expectancy for insurance products, an increase in life expectancy for annuity products, or an increase in the costs of administering products.
C-3 risk (interest-rate risk)	The risk that market interest rates might shift, causing the insurer's assets to lose value and/or its liabilities to gain value. Examples of C-3 risk include loss of asset value because of interest-rate increases, loss on the forced sale of assets or withdrawals by customers when interest rates increase, and losses related to bond prepayments or mortgage prepayments when interest rates decrease. Note that C-1 risk includes the risk of default, but does not include the risk of interest-rate changes, which is a C-3 risk.
C-4 risk (general management risk)	A risk of losses resulting from the insurer's ineffective general business practices, the need to pay a special assessment to cover another insurer's unsound business practices, unfavorable regulatory changes, or unfavorable changes in tax laws. Examples of C-4 risk include market risk from expansion into new lines or business or new markets; changes in laws affecting insurance business; fraud by employees, agents, or customers; mismanagement; and withdrawals by customers who fear insolvency.

- The ***financial condition examination*** is intended to identify and monitor any threats to the insurer's solvency.

- The ***market conduct examination*** is intended to verify that, in its dealings with customers, the insurer is complying with all applicable statutes and regulations regarding sales, advertising, underwriting, and claims.

In most states, each insurer domiciled in the state must be examined routinely once every three to five years. Each insurance commissioner has the discretion to have an insurer examined at shorter intervals. For any insurer operating in more than one specified geographic area or in more than three states, the NAIC recommends that the insurer receive an association examination. An **association examination** is an onsite regulatory examination that conforms to the procedures outlined in the NAIC's *Examiners Handbook*, which describes standard procedures for performing either a financial condition examination or a market conduct examination.

Here, we focus on the financial condition examination. Financial condition examinations are designed to investigate two broad aspects of an insurer's operations:

- Whether the insurer's accounting records are accurate and the insurer is being operated on a sound and lawful basis

- Whether the insurer's financial and business profiles contain any apparent hazards to the insurer's solvency

Each state specifies the requirements for routine onsite financial condition examinations of insurers. Most financial condition examinations are classified as association examinations. For an association examination, employees of a state's insurance department, called *examiners*, visit the insurer's home office and examine the soundness of the insurer's financial accounts and records, operating procedures, business plans, and management. In conducting a financial condition examination, examiners verify the operating results reported in the insurer's U.S. Annual Statement. Inaccurate financial records may conceal financial problems or unlawful activities.

State examiners also review other factors that help them evaluate whether the insurer is being operated soundly and in compliance with the law. For example, examiners might perform a broad-based analysis of the insurer's financial accounts and lines of business, or they might focus their analysis on specified problem areas, as identified from the insurer's Annual Statement, IRIS ratios, the FAST system, previous examinations, or any other source. In addition, examiners sometimes review the following factors:

- The liquidity, riskiness, and diversification of the insurer's asset portfolio

- The nature, riskiness, and diversification of the insurer's in-force business

- The adequacy of the insurer's reserves

- The insurer's expenses, particularly distribution expenses

- The insurer's capital position

Examination results are summarized in a document called an *examination report.* The examination report is submitted to both state regulators and the insurance company's officers. The examination report emphasizes any adverse conditions the examiners discover and any significant changes in the insurer's operations or financial condition since the last report. The examination report must at least identify and report any problems uncovered during the most recent examination. The report may also offer explanations of the causes of problems and suggestions for how the insurer might correct the problems. The NAIC *Examiners Handbook* presents a selection of topics that should be discussed in the examination report.

Regulatory Monitoring in Canada

The Office of the Superintendent of Financial Institutions (OSFI), a branch of the federal government, is responsible for monitoring federally licensed insurers in Canada. In addition, provincial departments of insurance monitor insurers licensed in those provinces. Some provinces have an arrangement with OSFI whereby OSFI examines insurers licensed in those provinces.

The Canadian Annual Return is often used for regulatory monitoring of solvency in Canada. Recall that the Canadian Annual Return is a financial report that insurers in Canada file with OSFI and the appropriate provincial regulatory authorities. Besides reviewing the Annual Return, Canadian regulators apply the following tools for routine regulatory monitoring:

- Scenario analysis

- The Minimum Continuing Capital and Surplus Requirements (MCCSR)

- Onsite regulatory examinations

Scenario Analysis

Insurers in Canada use a specific type of scenario analysis to comply with regulatory requirements. **Dynamic capital adequacy testing (DCAT)**, previously known as *dynamic solvency testing*, employs simulation modeling to project, as of a given valuation date, an insurance company's existing and future business, and to compare the amounts of assets, liabilities, and owners' equity at various times after the valuation date. The purpose of DCAT is to help an insurer to identify plausible

- Threats against the insurer's capital adequacy

- Actions to reduce the likelihood that capital-adequacy risk would occur

- Actions to minimize any loss if such a threat materialized

Minimum Continuing Capital and Surplus Requirements

Federally registered insurers in Canada must comply with the Minimum Continuing Capital and Surplus Requirements in order to continue insurance operations. Quebec-licensed insurers must meet a slightly different set of requirements that are similar to the federal requirements. The *Minimum Continuing Capital and Surplus Requirements (MCCSR)* were created by the Canadian Life and Health Insurance Association (CLHIA) and are enforced by OSFI in cooperation with CompCorp, the Canadian guaranty association. The MCCSR allows regulators to evaluate the adequacy of an insurer's capital and to provide an early warning tool for measuring insurer solvency.

Both the NAIC's RBC requirements in the United States and the MCCSR in Canada assume that the more risky an insurer's assets or products are, the more capital and surplus the insurer must maintain to offset that additional risk. The MCCSR formula is similar, but not identical, to the RBC formula. Thus, the MCCSR ratios are not equivalent to the RBC ratios. Moreover, the methods of calculating minimum capital amounts differ substantially between MCCSR and the NAIC-sponsored RBC. The MCCSR formula requires insurers to calculate adjusted financial statement values for the following four risk categories:

- Asset risk

- Pricing risk, which includes mortality risk, morbidity risk, lapse risk, and interest-margin pricing risk

- Interest-rate risk

- Segregated fund risk

The first three MCCSR risks listed here—asset risk, pricing risk, and interest-rate risk—roughly correspond to three of the C risks used for the NAIC's RBC purposes. The methods used to calculate asset risk and pricing risk under MCCSR are somewhat similar to the methods used in applying the C-1 and C-2 risk factors for the RBC calculation. In Canada, interest-rate risk is equivalent to C-3 risk. However, many of the risk-adjustment factors used for MCCSR calculations differ from the exact risk-adjustment percentages applied for RBC calculations.

The fourth risk category under MCCSR—segregated fund risk—is quite different from the NAIC's RBC requirements. **Segregated fund risk** is the risk associated with providing guarantees for segregated fund products. Recall that *segregated funds* is the Canadian term for U.S. *separate accounts.*

Onsite Regulatory Examinations

Although Canadian regulatory examinations of insurers are similar to U.S. examinations of financial condition, there are some differences. Notably, unlike U.S. regulatory examinations, Canadian regulatory examinations do not verify the accuracy of the insurer's financial records. Instead, Canadian examinations rely completely on the insurer's external auditors for financial verification, and then concentrate on evaluating any solvency risks.

Also, before an onsite visit, Canadian examiners use a set of **early-warning financial ratio tests,** similar to the IRIS ratio tests used in the United States. Canadian examiners analyze an insurer's financial statements, apply these early-warning ratios, and take note of any other information available. Examiners then create a customized examination plan that is designed to focus the onsite examination on the risks identified from the insurer's financial information. During the examination, the examiners follow the customized examination plan. They analyze the factors that are frequently mentioned as potential threats to an insurer's solvency: capital and surplus adequacy, asset quality, asset liquidity, reserve sufficiency, the match of assets to liabilities, and the insurer's corresponding interest-rate risk.

Figure 10-3 summarizes our discussion of regulatory solvency surveillance tools in the United States and Canada.

FIGURE 10-3. Routine Regulatory Monitoring of Insurance Company Solvency.

United States	Canada
Annual Statement information	*Annual Return* information
IRIS ratios	Early-warning financial ratio tests
FAST System	
Scenario testing (CFT, DFA)	Scenario testing (DCAT)
Risk-based capital (RBC) ratio monitoring	Minimum Continuing Capital and Surplus Requirements (MCCSR)
Onsite regulatory examinations	Onsite regulatory examinations

Key Terms and Concepts

Insurance Regulatory
Information System
(IRIS) ratios
Financial Analysis and
Solvency Tracking
(FAST) system
scenario analysis
cash-flow testing (CFT)
dynamic financial
analysis (DFA)
risk-based capital (RBC)
requirements
C risks
C-1 risk (asset risk)
C-2 risk (pricing risk)
C-3 risk (interest-rate risk)
C-4 risk (general
management risk)

onsite regulatory
examination
financial condition
examination
market conduct examination
association examination
examination report
dynamic capital adequacy
testing (DCAT)
Minimum Continuing Capital
and Surplus Requirements
(MCCSR)
segregated fund risk
early-warning financial
ratio tests

Glossary

account form. The presentation format of a balance sheet in which asset accounts appear on the left side and liabilities and owners' equity accounts appear on the right side. [1]

account payable. A liability account that represents a promise of payment by the insurer to another party. [2]

account receivable. An asset account that represents a contractual promise by another party to pay the insurer. [2]

accounting entry. A record of a financial transaction that (1) includes at least one debit and one credit and (2) shows the monetary value of the transaction in balance on a specified date. [2]

accrual-basis accounting. The accounting basis under which a company records revenues when they are earned and expenses when they are incurred, even if the company has not yet received the revenues or paid the expenses. [7]

accrued income. Income that the insurer has already earned, but which is not receivable until a specified date in the next accounting period—that is, income that is due after the insurer's financial reporting date. [3]

accumulated cost of insurance. The net single premium needed to provide benefit payments for those who have died. [4]

accumulated value of net premiums. The total of net premiums collected, accumulated at interest. [4]

acquisition expenses. The costs of obtaining and issuing new business. [8]

active life reserves. *See* **claim reserves.**

activity ratios. Financial ratios, measuring the speed with which various assets are converted into sales or cash, that gauge the productivity and efficiency of a company. [9]

actuarial assumption. Each assumed value used in life insurance product design. [4]

actuary. An expert in the mathematics of insurance, annuities, and financial instruments. [4]

admitted assets. Assets whose full value can be reported on the Assets page of the U.S. Annual Statement. [2]

advance premiums. *See* **premiums paid in advance.**

amortization. The accounting process by which an insurer periodically and systematically decreases the original cost of an investment to its ultimate value at maturity. [2]

amortized cost. An asset's historical cost, less any adjustment, such as depreciation or amortization, to the asset's book value. [2]

annual report. A document that a company's management sends to its stockholders and other interested parties to report on the company's financial performance during the past year. [1]

Annual Return. A financial report that every insurer in Canada must file with the Office of the Superintendent of Financial Institutions (OSFI) and with the insurance regulatory organization in each province in which the insurer conducts business. [1]

Annual Statement. A financial report that every insurer in the United States must file annually, as well as on a quarterly basis, with the National Association of Insurance Commissioners (NAIC) and the insurance regulatory organization in each state in which the insurer conducts business. [1]

apportioned dividends. *See* **policyowner dividends payable in the following year.**

appropriated surplus. *See* **special surplus.**

asset risk. *See* **C-1 risk (asset risk).**

assets. All items, generally of readily determined monetary value, that a company owns. [1]

assigned surplus. *See* **special surplus.**

association examination. An onsite regulatory examination that conforms to the procedures outlined in the National Association of Insurance Commissioners' [NAIC's] Examiners Handbook, which outlines standard procedures for performing either a financial condition examination or a market conduct examination. [10]

assuming company. *See* **reinsurer.**

assumption reinsurance. A reinsurance agreement designed to transfer blocks of existing insurance business permanently and entirely from one insurance company to another. [6]

balance sheet. A financial statement that shows an insurer's financial condition or position as of a specified date. [1]

balance sheet equation. *See* **basic accounting equation.**

bank reconciliation. The process of identifying and explaining the difference between (1) the balance presented on the bank statement and (2) the balance in the insurer's accounting records, sometimes referred to as the book balance. [3]

base period. The earliest financial reporting period used in horizontal analysis. [9]

basic accounting equation. A mathematical depiction of the relationship among the three key account classifications—assets, liabilities, and owners' equity—on the balance sheet. [1]

bond. A debt security issued by a borrower. [2]

bond issuer. The entity that sells the bond to raise money. [2]

bond principal. An amount of money originally borrowed; the designated legal monetary value assigned to each bond—generally $1,000. [2]

bondholder. The owner of a bond. [2]

bonus additions. In Canada, applications of the policyowner dividend payout options to purchase paid-up additions or one-year term insurance. [5]

book balance. *See* **bank reconciliation.**

book value. An asset's original cost—adjusted for capitalized acquisition costs, accumulated depreciation, and other specified amounts—and recorded in a company's accounting records. [2]

C risks. Four specific contingency risks, included in the risk-based capital (RBC) formula, that the National Association of Insurance Commissioners (NAIC) uses to evaluate an insurer's total risk. [10]

C-1 risk (asset risk). The risk that an insurer will lose asset value on its invested assets, such as stocks, bonds, mortgages, and real estate. [10]

C-2 risk (pricing risk). The risk that an insurer's experience with mortality or expenses will differ significantly from expectations, causing the insurer to lose money on its products. [10]

C-3 risk (interest-rate risk). The risk that market interest rates might shift, causing the insurer's assets to lose value and/or its liabilities to gain value. [10]

C-4 risk (general management risk). The risk of losses resulting from the insurer's ineffective general business practices, the need to pay a special assessment to cover another insurer's unsound business practices, unfavorable regulatory changes, or unfavorable changes in tax laws. [10]

Canadian Life and Health Insurance Compensation Corporation (CompCorp). An organization, similar to state guaranty associations in the United States, that protects policyowners and beneficiaries throughout Canada. [8]

capital. The money that an insurer's owners have invested in the insurer. [6]

capital and surplus ratios. Financial ratios used to express the relationship between an insurer's capital and surplus and its liabilities. [9]

capital gain. The amount by which the selling price of an asset exceeds its purchase price. [2]

capital loss. The amount by which the purchase price of an asset exceeds its selling price. [2]

capital ratios. *See* **capital and surplus ratios.**

capitalization ratios. *See* **capital and surplus ratios.**

capitalize. To record an expense, such as deferred acquisition costs, as an asset. [3]

cash. The amount of currency on hand or on deposit at an insurer's bank. [2]

cash accounting. The management and maintenance of records for, and the reporting of, all cash transactions, specifically money deposited or withdrawn from an insurer's accounts at a bank or other financial institution. [3]

cash-basis accounting. The accounting basis under which a company recognizes revenues or expenses only when the company receives or disburses cash. [7]

cash dividend on stock. A cash payment that a company distributes periodically to the owners of its preferred stock and common stock. [2]

cash equivalents. Short-term assets that are not cash, but can typically be converted to cash within 90 days with little or no risk of losing value. [2]

cash flow statement. A financial statement that provides information about the company's cash inflows and cash outflows during a specified period. [1]

cash-flow testing [CFT]. A type of scenario analysis that involves projecting the cash flows associated with an insurer's existing business and comparing the timing and amounts of cash flows for assets and liabilities after the valuation date. [10]

cash inflow. A source of funds, such as cash receipts from policy premiums, investment income, and fee income. [1]

cash management. *See* **cash accounting.**

cash outflow. A use of funds, such as cash disbursements paid for policy benefits, investment purchases, and business expenses. [1]

cash surrender value. The amount of money that a policyowner will receive on a specified date if the policyowner terminates the coverage and surrenders the policy to the insurer. [3]

ceding company. The insurance company that transfers some of its insurance risk to a reinsurer. [4]

certificate loan. *See* **policy loan.**

CFT. *See* **cash-flow testing.**

claim reserves. The liability accounts that identify the future amounts that an insurer will pay on claims that have been reported to the insurer before the date of the financial statement but have not yet been paid in full as of that date. Claim reserves typically consist of disabled life reserves and active life reserves. [4]

CMOs. *See* **collateralized mortgage obligations.**

collateral. Something of value, generally a portion of the bond issuer's assets, which the bondholder will receive if the bond issuer fails to make the contracted interest and principal payments on the bond. [2]

collateralized mortgage obligations (CMOs). Mortgage-backed bonds that are secured by a pool of residential mortgage loans. [2]

collected income. The amount of income received in cash during a reporting period, including certain adjustments. [7]

commission. Monetary compensation paid to a sales producer, usually expressed as a percentage of the gross premiums paid by customers. [5]

common-size financial statement. A financial statement that consists of the percentages obtained from vertical analysis. [9]

common stock. A unit of ownership that usually entitles the owner to vote on the selection of directors and on other important company matters and also entitles the owner to receive dividends on the stock. [2]

comparative financial statements. Financial statements that present a company's financial information for two or more accounting periods. [9]

CompCorp. *See* **Canadian Life and Health Insurance Compensation Corporation.**

contingency reserves. *See* **special surplus.**

contingency risks. *See* **C risks.**

contra account. An account that accompanies a specified "companion" account—typically an asset account—and that has a normal balance that is the opposite of the companion account. [3]

contractual payments. Payments on supplementary contracts. [5]

contractual reserves. Accounting liabilities that identify the amount that, together with future premiums and interest earnings, represents the expected amount of future benefits payable on an insurer's in-force business—that is, the insurer's obligations to its customers. Called required reserves, provision for future policy benefits, or net actuarial liabilities in Canada. [4]

control account. An accounting entry that serves as a summary of the monetary amounts of expenses that are reported in a company's financial statements. [8]

corporate bonds. Bonds issued by a corporation. [2]

credit. A specified change made to the monetary value of an account that increases the value of liability accounts, owners' equity accounts, and revenue accounts, whereas it decreases the value of asset accounts and expense accounts. [2]

cumulative dividends. A type of preferred stock dividend arrangement in which a company must pay in full any unpaid scheduled dividends on its preferred stock before it may pay any dividends on its common stock. [6]

current assets. *See* **short-term assets.**

current market value. The price at which an asset can be sold under current economic conditions. [2]

DAC. *See* **deferred acquisition costs.**

DCAT. *See* **dynamic capital adequacy testing.**

death claim. A request for payment, upon the death of the insured, under the terms and conditions of a life insurance policy. [5]

debenture. An unsecured corporate bond. [2]

debit. A specified change made to the monetary value of an account that increases the value of asset accounts and expense accounts, whereas it decreases the value of liability accounts, owners' equity accounts, and revenue accounts. [2]

debt assets. Assets that represent an investor's loan of funds to the debt issuer in return for the promised repayment of principal and payment of interest. [2]

debt-to-surplus ratio. A financial ratio, calculated by dividing total liabilities by total surplus, that measures the relationship between a company's liabilities and its surplus. [9]

deferred acquisition costs (DAC). Costs reported under U.S. GAAP that are related primarily and directly to acquiring new business and retaining current business associated with new insurance products. [3]

deferred income. Premium income due after the U.S. Annual Statement reporting date, but before the next policy anniversary date. [7]

deferred policy acquisition costs (DPAC). *See* **deferred acquisition costs (DAC).**

deferred premiums. Life insurance premiums due after the date of the U.S. Annual Statement but before the next policy anniversary date and the next Annual Statement date. [3]

demutualization. The process of converting a mutual insurance company to a stock insurance company. [6]

deposits in transit. *See* **unrecorded deposits.**

depreciation. The accounting process of allocating (spreading) the cost of an asset over the asset's estimated useful life. [2]

derivatives. Financial assets whose values are based on other securities such as stocks or bonds. [3]

development expenses. The expenses related to starting a new product or line of business [8]

DFA. *See* **dynamic financial analysis.**

disabled life reserves. *See* **claim reserves.**

discount. The difference between a bond's current market value and its principal, when the current market value is lower than the bond's principal. [2]

dividend accumulations. The election, by a policyowner, to leave policyowner dividends on deposit at interest with the insurer. [5]

dividend on stock. A share of a company's earnings that the company pays to its stockholders. [2]

dividend payment options. *See* **policyowner dividend payment options.**

divisible surplus. *See* **unassigned surplus.**

DPAC. *See* **deferred acquisition costs.**

due income. Income that was expected by the insurer before the financial reporting date but that has not yet been received. [3]

due premiums. Group life insurance premiums that are due before December 31, but which the insurer has not received as of December 31. [7]

dynamic capital adequacy testing. A type of scenario analysis, used by insurers in Canada, that employs simulation modeling to project, as of a given valuation date, the insurer's existing and future business, and to compare the amounts of the insurer's assets, liabilities, and owners' equity at various times after the valuation date. [10]

dynamic financial analysis (DFA). A type of scenario analysis, broader in scope than cash-flow testing, in which insurers use simulation modeling and multiple-scenario testing to project future values for an insurer's assets, liabilities, and owners' equity. [10]

dynamic solvency testing. *See* **dynamic capital adequacy testing (DCAT).**

early-warning financial ratio tests. A set of financial ratios that Canadian examiners use to analyze an insurer's financial statements and to create a customized examination plan that is designed to focus the onsite regulatory examination on the risks identified from the insurer's financial information. [10]

earmarked surplus. *See* **special surplus.**

effective rate of return. The actual rate of return on the amount paid for a bond. Generally, the effective rate of return on a bond is higher than the stated rate of return for a bond purchased at a discount and lower than the stated rate of return for a bond purchased at a premium. [2]

effective yield. *See* **effective rate of return.**

equity assets. Assets that represent an investor's ownership or share of ownership in an asset such as a business or property. [2]

escrow account. A trust account used to pay property maintenance expenses, property taxes, and other expenses related to a mortgaged property. [2]

examination report. A document, summarizing examination results and noting any adverse conditions or significant changes in an insurer's operations or financial condition, that is submitted to both state regulators and the insurer's officers. [10]

ex-date. *See* **ex-dividend date.**

ex-dividend date. The date that determines whether a stockholder is eligible to receive a declared cash dividend. [2]

expenses. The amounts of one or more assets that a company uses to receive benefits, goods, or services. [1]

external analysis. Financial ratio analysis performed by someone outside of the company being analyzed. [9]

face amount. *See* **bond principal.**

face value. *See* **bond principal.**

fair market value. *See* **current market value.**

FAST system. *See* **Financial Analysis and Solvency Tracking system.**

financial accounting. The field of accounting that focuses primarily on reporting a company's financial information to meet the needs of the company's external users. [1]

Financial Analysis and Solvency Tracking (FAST) system. A specified type of financial analysis in which insurance regulators in the United States examine a large insurer's solvency using (1) ratio analysis of the insurer's most recent financial statements, and (2) an analysis of the five-year history of specific aspects of the insurer's financial statements. [10]

financial condition examination. The part of an onsite regulatory examination used by insurance regulators to identify and monitor any threats to the insurer's solvency. [10]

financial leverage. The effect whereby incurring fixed financing costs—usually borrowed funds—automatically magnifies a company's risks and potential returns. [9]

financial ratio. A percentage amount that expresses a relationship between two pieces of financial information. [9]

financial ratio analysis. The process of calculating the relationships between various pairs of financial statement values for the purpose of assessing a company's financial condition or performance. [9]

financial statements. Standardized reports that summarize a company's major financial events and transactions. [1]

financing activities. Transactions that involve borrowed funds and cash payments to or from a company's owners. [1]

fixed dividends. Preferred stock dividend payments that are fixed in both schedule and amount. [6]

foreclosure. A legal procedure by which a lender recovers the unpaid loan balance by obtaining title to the real estate offered as collateral if the borrower fails to make timely contractual principal and interest payments on the loan. [3]

forward contracts. Limited-time agreements that give the owner the right to buy or sell a specified investment in the future for a stated price. [3]

free surplus. *See* **unassigned surplus.**

futures contracts. Limited-time agreements that give the owner the right to buy or sell a specified investment in the future for a stated price. [3]

GAAP. *See* **generally accepted accounting principles (GAAP).**

GAAP accounting records. Accounting records, designed for financial reporting to investors and the public at large, that focus on showing the company's financial stability along with its profitability. [4]

gain. Any income that insurer obtains from a transaction outside its core business operations. [6]

general account. The portfolio of assets backing an insurer's guaranteed products, such as whole life insurance and fixed-rate annuities. [3]

general and administrative expenses. The costs, incurred as a result of an insurer's normal business operations, that include both (1) contractual benefit expenses and (2) operating expenses. [8]

general management risk. *See* **C-4 risk.**

generally accepted accounting principles (GAAP). A set of financial accounting standards that all publicly traded companies in the United States and all companies in Canada follow when preparing their financial statements. [1]

government bonds. Bonds issued by governments—including federal, state, provincial, county, city, and local governments. [2]

gross investment income. Total investment income actually earned, on an accrual-basis and before deducting expenses and amortization, during a specified reporting period. [7]

gross leverage ratio. *See* **insurance leverage ratio.**

gross paid-in and contributed surplus. Under statutory accounting practices, the aggregate amount paid above the par value for shares of the stock of a insurer in the United States. [6]

gross profit ratio. A financial ratio, developed by the A.M. Best Company, that compares an insurer's contributions to capital during a reporting period to its beginning capital and surplus for the period. [9]

gross reserve valuation method. A method of computing reserves that makes explicit provision for the insurer's product-related expenses or loading. [4]

gross reserves. Reserves developed using a gross reserve valuation method. [4]

guaranty-fund assessments. Charges payable by sound insurers to the unsupported customer obligations of a failed insurer that had operated in a jurisdiction where the surviving insurer does business. [8]

hedging. A strategy of investing in a given asset in order to reduce the overall riskiness of a given portfolio's asset mix. [3]

historical cost. The purchase price originally paid for an asset. [2]

horizontal analysis. A type of financial ratio analysis that involves calculating the absolute amount and the percentage of the increase or decrease in a specified financial statement from one reporting period to another. [9]

income accounts. *See* **revenue accounts.**

income statement. A financial statement that (1) reports an insurer's revenues and expenses during a specified period and (2) indicates whether the insurer experienced net income or a net loss during the period. [1]

index number. In trend analysis, a number that provides a statistical method for measuring the change in a variable. [9]

index-number trend analysis. *See* **trend analysis.**

insolvency. The inability of an insurer to pay its financial obligations on time. [6]

insurance leverage ratio. A financial ratio that compares an insurer's contractual reserves with its capital and surplus. [9]

Insurance Regulatory Information System (IRIS) ratios. The set of specific financial ratios, developed by the National Association of Insurance Commissioners (NAIC) and the A.M. Best Company, that insurance regulators in the United States use to monitor life insurance companies. [10]

intangible assets. Assets that represent ownership of a legal right or another nonphysical resource. [2]

interest payment. The monetary amount of income that a bond issuer pays on the bond to the bondholder. [2]

interest-rate risk. *See* **C-3 risk.**

interest-rate swaps. A specific type of swap, in which two parties agree to exchange a set of cash flows, typically with one based on a fixed interest rate and the other based on a floating interest rate. [3]

intermediate term. A term to maturity from one to ten years (United States) or a term to maturity from six years to ten years (Canada). [2]

internal accounting records. Accounting records designed for financial reporting to company management, whose main interest is in having appropriate data for making decisions. [4]

internal analysis. Financial ratio analysis undertaken by employees of the company being analyzed. [9]

invested assets. The debt securities, equity securities, and derivative securities purchased by an insurer to generate earnings. [2]

investing. The process of employing a principal sum of money—usually to purchase assets or place a sum on deposit—to generate earnings. [2]

investing activities. Transactions that involve a company's purchase or sale of long-term assets and the lending of long-term funds to other companies. [1]

investment expenses. The costs associated with investing an insurer's assets. [8]

investment risk. The risk of losing some or all of an original investment or failing to earn some or all of an expected return on an investment. [3]

investment yield ratio. A financial ratio, comparing an insurer's investment income to the insurer's average invested assets for the period, that shows how efficiently an insurer has used its invested assets to earn a return. [9]

investments. *See* **invested assets.**

IRIS ratios. *See* **Insurance Regulatory Information System ratios.**

issue strain. *See* **surplus strain.**

LCM rule. *See* **lower of cost or market rule.**

legal reserves. *See* **contractual reserves.**

leverage. *See* **leverage effect.**

leverage effect. A financial effect in which the presence of fixed costs—either operating costs or financing costs—automatically magnifies the potential risks and returns to the company's owners. [9]

leverage ratios. Financial ratios that compare the amount of an insurer's obligations with the insurer's ability to meet those obligations. [9]

liabilities. The account classification that represents a company's monetary values for its current and future obligations. [1]

LICTI. *See* **life insurance company taxable income.**

life insurance company taxable income (LICTI). The difference between a life insurance company's gross income and its tax deductions. To calculate LICTI, insurers first determine gross income, which includes advance premiums and excludes deferred and uncollected premiums. [8]

liquid assets. An insurer's cash and readily marketable assets. [9]

liquidity. The ease with which an asset can be converted into cash for an approximation of its true value. [2]

liquidity ratios. Financial ratios that measure a company's ability to meet its maturing short-term obligations. [9]

long term. A term to maturity that covers a period greater than ten years (United States and Canada). [2]

long-term assets. Assets that a company expects to hold indefinitely or for a long time—generally more than one year—to generate income. [2]

loss. The result when an insurer loses money on a transaction that is outside the insurer's core business operations. [6]

lower of cost or market (LCM) rule. Under statutory accounting practices, a bond's monetary value is defined as either its amortized cost or its current market value, whichever is lower. [2]

maintenance expenses. Product-related costs, including renewal commissions and ongoing customer service costs, that are incurred after an insurance contract is in force. [8]

margin. In the context of leverage, the difference between the cost of borrowing the funds and the return earned using these funds. [9]

marginal return. *See* **margin.**

market conduct examination. The part of an onsite regulatory examination used by insurance regulators to verify that, in its dealings with customers, the insurer is complying with all applicable statutes and regulations regarding sales, advertising, underwriting, and claims. [10]

maturity date. The date on which the bond issuer must repay to the bondholder the amount originally borrowed. [2]

maturity value. *See* **bond principal.**

MCCSR. *See* **Minimum Continuing Capital and Surplus Requirements.**

Minimum Continuing Capital and Surplus Requirements (MCCSR). A set of risk-based capital requirements, created by the Canadian Life and Health Insurance Association (CLHIA) and enforced by the Office of the Superintendent of Financial Institutions (OSFI) in cooperation with CompCorp, that allows regulators to evaluate the adequacy of an insurer's capital and to provide an early warning tool for measuring the solvency of insurers in Canada. [10]

modified GAAP accounting records. *See* **internal accounting records.**

modified reserve. A reserve developed using a modified reserve valuation method. [4]

modified reserve valuation method. A method of calculating U.S. statutory reserves that permits an insurer to set a lower-than-level first-year contractual reserve in recognition of the surplus strain from a product's first-year expenses. [4]

mortgage. A loan secured by a pledge of specified real property. [2]

moving average market method. A process in which an insurer in Canada systematically adjusts unrealized gains or losses that result from changes in the current market value of equity investments over a period of years. [2]

negative leverage effect. The effect of earning a lower profit because of the presence of leverage. [9]

net actuarial liabilities. *See* **contractual reserves.**

net book value. An asset's historical cost less accumulated depreciation only. [2]

net cash value. *See* **cash surrender value.**

net change in cash. An increase or decrease in cash during an accounting period. [1]

net GAAP reserves. An insurer's GAAP reserves minus its deferred acquisition costs (DAC). [4]

net gain to total income ratio. A financial ratio that measure an insurer's share of operating income—that is, operating income minus operating expenses—that represents the insurer's net income. [9]

net income. The result if a company's revenues for a reporting period exceed its expenses for the period. [1]

net investment income. The amount of investment income that remains after deducting expenses and amortization from gross investment income. [7]

net level premium approach. An approach to estimating contractual reserves that assumes that the amount of a policy's net premiums does not increase or decrease during the life of the policy. [4]

net loss. The result if a company's expenses for a reporting period exceed its revenues for the period. [1]

net reserve valuation method. A method of computing reserves that does not make explicit provision for the insurer's product-related expenses or loading. [4]

net reserves. Reserves developed using a net reserve valuation method. [4]

net single premium. The actuarial present value at policy issue of a product's future benefit costs. [4]

net yield. *See* **investment yield ratio.**

new business strain. *See* **surplus strain.**

nonadmitted assets. Assets whose values are accorded no value on the Assets page of the U.S. Annual Statement. [2]

nonadmitted income. For insurers in the United States, income that is overdue for more than a specified period—such as three months to two years—as prescribed by state insurance laws. [7]

noncontractual reserves. Insurers' business obligations that are not directly attributable to paying benefit for a specified product. All types of reserves that are not contractual are classified as noncontractual reserves. [4]

noncurrent assets. *See* **long-term assets.**

nonforfeiture options. The various ways in which a policyowner can apply the policy's cash surrender value of a life insurance policy or an annuity if the insurance contract lapses. [5]

nonforfeiture values. The benefits that the insurer guarantees to a policyowner if an insurance contract lapses. [5]

nonsufficient funds (NSF) checks. Checks that have "bounced;" in other words, the payor did not have enough money in its checking account to pay the amount of the check. [3]

normal balance. Whether a debit or a credit to an account increases the account's monetary value. [2]

NSF checks. *See* **nonsufficient funds checks.**

on account. An asset purchase in which the insurer promises to pay to the seller in the future. [2]

onsite regulatory examination. A tool that insurance regulators use to monitor the solvency of insurers. [10]

operating activities. Transactions that involve a company's major lines of business and that directly determine the company's net income. [1]

operating efficiency ratios. *See* **activity ratios.**

operating expenses. The expenses, other than contractual benefit expenses, that arise in the normal course of conducting business, and that include (1) acquisition expenses, (2) development expenses, (3) maintenance expenses, and (4) overhead expenses. [8]

operating leverage. The effect whereby incurring fixed operating costs automatically magnifies a company's risks and potential returns. [9]

options. Limited-time contracts that give the owner the right to either buy or sell a specified asset for a stated price. [3]

outstanding checks. Checks that the insurer has written, deducted from its book balance, and sent to payees, but which have not yet cleared the bank. [3]

overhead. *See* **overhead expenses.**

overhead costs. *See* **overhead expenses.**

overhead expenses. The costs, incurred during normal business operations, that are not directly related to a specified product or service. [8]

owners' equity. The owners' investment in a company. [1]

par value (of a bond). *See* **bond principal.**

par value of stock. The designated legal value assigned to each outstanding share of common stock. [2]

partially admitted assets. Assets for which only a portion of their monetary value can be reported on the Assets page of the U.S. Annual Statement. [2]

personal property. Any property that is not real estate. [3]

policy accounting. *See* **premium accounting.**

policy loan. A loan made to a policyowner and secured by a policy's cash surrender value as collateral. [3]

policy premium method (PPM). In Canada, a type of prospective gross reserve valuation method in which the contractual reserve is equal to the difference between the present value of future benefits and the present value of future gross premiums. [4]

policy reserves. *See* **contractual reserves.**

policyholder dividend. *See* **policyowner dividend.**

policyowner dividend. The portion of an insurer's surplus that is paid to participating policyowners and is considered a partial refund of the policy premium that was not needed by the insurer for policy expenses. [5]

policyowner dividend liabilities. Accounts that represent all policyowner dividends that have been declared by an insurer's board of directors, but which have not yet been paid to policyowners. [5]

policyowner dividend payment options. Applications that enable participating policyowners to select the manner in which they want their policyowner dividends disbursed. [5]

policyowner dividends due and unpaid. Policyowner dividends that were declared by an insurer's board of directors during the year, but that have not yet been paid as of the current financial statement date. [5]

policyowner dividends payable in the following year. The estimated amount of all policyowner dividends that an insurance company's board of directors has declared that are payable in the following calendar year or policy year. [5]

portfolio. A collection of various assets assembled for the purpose of meeting a defined set of investment goals. [2]

positive leverage effect. The effect of earning a higher profit as a result of leverage. [9]

PPM. *See* **policy premium method.**

preferred stock. A unit of ownership that typically does not carry the voting rights of common stock, but does carry a stated dividend rate or monetary amount that has a priority over that of dividends on common stock. [2]

premium. In the context of bonds, the excess of a bond's current market value over its principal. [2]

premium accounting. The accounting process that encompasses the maintenance of detailed accounting records and reports of insurance policy transactions. [7]

premium deposits. Amounts that an insurer's policyowners leave on deposit with the insurer to pay for future premiums. [5]

premium suspense account. A liability account used to record transactions that are intended as premiums but which the insurer cannot accept as income until a particular event occurs. [5]

premium taxes. The taxes on an insurer's premium income earned within a state or province. [8]

premiums outstanding. *See* **uncollected premiums.**

premiums paid in advance. A liability account that an insurer establishes when an insured pays a premium in one accounting period for coverage that does not begin until the next policy anniversary. [5]

prepaid expenses. Those expenditures, remitted in advance, that the insurer expects will provide a future value or benefit. [3]

present value of future benefits. The net single premium at the insured's attained age for the remaining policy benefits. [4]

present value of future net premiums. The present value of a life annuity due. [4]

pricing risk. *See* **C-2 risk.**

profit. *See* **net income.**

profit margin. *See* **margin.**

profitability. The degree to which a company is successful in consistently generating returns to its owners. [6]

profitability ratios. Financial ratios that measure a company's profitability by comparing the company's gain from operations to the resources employed or invested to earn the gain. [9]

property. An asset that can be owned or possessed. [3]

prospective reserve valuation method. A way of estimating a value for a contractual reserve liability that involves finding the present value of a contract's future cash flows—its future premiums and future benefit payments. [4]

provision for adverse deviation. In the United States, a safety margin that allows for unfavorable variations from an insurer's actuarial assumptions. [4]

provision for future policy benefits. *See* **contractual reserves.**

quick liquidity ratio. A financial ratio, comparing an insurer's liquid assets to its contractual reserves, that indicates the insurer's ability to make contractual benefit payments without having to sell its long-term invested assets or borrow money. [9]

rate of return. A return that is expressed as a percentage relative to the invested principal. [2]

RBC requirements. *See* **risk-based requirements.**

real estate. Land or anything attached to the land. [3]

real property. *See* **real estate.**

realization principle. A revenue recognition concept under which a company recognizes revenues when they are earned, rather than when they are received, so long as a legal and reasonable expectation exists that the company's customer will remit payment in full. [7]

realized gain (loss). The difference between an asset's net sales proceeds and its book value. [2]

recognition. The process of recording a transaction in a company's accounting system as an asset, liability, owners' equity, revenue, or expense account. [7]

reinsurance. A transaction between two insurance companies in which the reinsurer agrees to take on (assume) some of the insurance risks of the ceding company. [4]

reinsurance commissions. Payments intended to cover all or part of a ceding company's acquisition costs and other costs related to reinsured business. [8]

reinsurer. The insurance company that assumes some of the insurance risks of a ceding company. [4]

released reserve. A contractual reserve that was originally established in connection with an in-force policy but is no longer required. [4]

report form. The presentation format of a balance sheet in which asset accounts, liability accounts, and owners' equity accounts are listed vertically. [1]

required reserves. *See* **contractual reserves.**

reserve credit. The solvency-basis accounting entry that a ceding company uses to record a reduction of reserves due to the use of reinsurance. [4]

reserve destrengthening. The process of decreasing the amount of reserves. [4]

reserve strengthening. The process of increasing the amount of reserves. [4]

reserve valuation method. An approach for calculating reserve amounts. [4]

reserves. Estimates of the amounts of money that an insurer needs to pay future business obligations. [4]

retained earnings. A GAAP account that represents the cumulative amount of a company's earnings that has been kept in the company over time to finance the company's ongoing operations. [6]

retaliatory tax laws. Laws that impose premium taxes on a foreign insurer, which is an insurer domiciled in another state, at the rate domestic companies in the state of domicile would be taxed by the foreign state, but only if the premium tax rate is higher in the state of domicile. [8]

retention limit. For a specified group of insureds or contracts, the maximum amount of coverage per life that an insurer will keep at its own risk, without ceding a portion of the risk to a reinsurer. [4]

retired stock. Stock that an insurer in the United States had previously issued, then later repurchased at market price, with no intention of reselling the stock at a later date. [6]

retrospective reserve valuation method. A way of estimating a value for a contractual reserve liability that involves finding the accumulated values of a contract's past cash flows—its past premiums and past benefit payments. [4]

return. The reward an investor hopes to receive for taking a risk. [2]

return on capital ratio. A financial ratio that indicates the percentage return an insurer has earned on its capital and surplus. [9]

revenue accounts. The accounts used to record and report a company's revenues. [7]

revenues. The amounts earned from a company's core business operations. [1]

risk. The possibility that an investor will fail to earn an expected return or will lose all or part of an investment. [2]

risk-based capital (RBC) requirements. The minimum capital level needed by an insurer of that insurer's size and risk profile, as identified by a specific National Association of Insurance Commissioners (NAIC) formula. [10]

risk-return trade-off. The direct relationship between risk and return: as risk increases, so does expected return. [2]

scenario analysis. A quantitative modeling technique that involves entering different sets of data into a model and then determining how changes in the input data affect the model's output. [10]

secured bond. A bond in which the issuer pledges something of value to guarantee the safety of the bondholder's investment. [2]

securities. Financial agreements representing evidence of the right to collect repayment of a loan, ownership of an asset, or the legal right to purchase or sell ownership of an asset. [2]

segregated account. *See* **separate account.**

segregated fund. *See* **separate account.**

segregated fund risk. In Canada, the risk associated with providing guarantees for segregated fund products. [10]

separate account. A separate portfolio that is used to support nonguaranteed insurance products—such as variable life insurance and variable annuities—in which the customer shares or assumes investment risk. Called a segregated fund or a segregated account in Canada. [3]

settlement contract. *See* **supplementary contract.**

shareholder. *See* **stockholder.**

short term. A term to maturity of less than one year (United States) or a term to maturity from zero years to six years (Canada). [2]

short-term assets. Assets that a company expects to convert to cash within one year. [2]

solvency. Generally, the ability of a company to meet its financial obligations on time. [6]

solvency-basis accounting records. *See* **statutory accounting records.**

special surplus. A part of an insurer's surplus that the insurer's board of directors has set aside to (1) meet unforeseen contingencies or (2) pay for certain extraordinary expenses. [6]

special surplus funds. *See* **special surplus.**

spread. *See* **margin.**

stated rate. The rate of interest specified on the bond certificate. [2]

statement of owners' equity. A financial statement that shows the changes that occurred in owners' equity during a specified period. [1]

statement of policyholders' equity. *See* **statement of owners' equity.**

statement of policyowners' equity. *See* **statement of owners' equity.**

statement of stockholders' equity. *See* **statement of owners' equity.**

statutory accounting practices. Accounting standards that all life insurers in the United States must follow when preparing the U.S. Annual Statement. [1]

statutory accounting records. Accounting records designed for financial reporting to state insurance regulators, whose primary interest is in evaluating insurance companies' solvency and long-term financial stability. [4]

statutory reserves. *See* **contractual reserves.**

stock. An asset that represents a stockholder's ownership interest in a company. [2]

stock dividend. A dividend that a company pays, in the form of additional shares of company stock, to its stockholders. [2]

stockholder. Anyone who owns shares of stock in a company. [2]

supplementary contract. The election of a settlement option by a life insurance beneficiary. [5]

surplus. Under statutory accounting practices, the cumulative monetary amount that remains in an insurance company over time. [6]

surplus note. A special type of unsecured debt security, issued only by insurance companies, that has characteristics of both traditional equity securities and traditional debt securities. [6]

surplus ratios. *See* **capital and surplus ratios.**

surplus relief. Any arrangement to diminish potential surplus strain. [4]

surplus relief ratio. A financial ratio that compares an insurer's net cost for ceding reinsurance or net earnings from assuming reinsurance to the insurer's capital and surplus. [9]

surplus strain. The decrease in an insurer's surplus caused by the high first-year costs and the reserving requirements associated with new products. [4]

suspense account. An account that an insurer uses to record transactions that cannot be credited immediately to a specified account. [5]

swaps. Limited-time agreements that give the owner the right to exchange the cash flow from one asset for the cash flow from another asset. [3]

tabular reserves. *See* **contractual reserves.**

tangible assets. Assets that have physical form. [2]

tax accounting records. Accounting records designed for financial reporting to taxation authorities in the United States and Canada. [4]

tentative LICTI. The amount of gross income minus deductible expenses before subtracting the small life insurance company deduction, excluding income from non-insurance operations. [8]

term to maturity. The amount of time that passes before an asset can be converted to cash for an approximation of its value. [2]

total asset turnover. An activity ratio that measures how efficiently a company has used its total assets to generate revenues. [9]

total leverage. The combined effect of operating leverage and financial leverage, representing the effect whereby incurring fixed operating costs and fixed financing costs automatically magnifies both risks and potential returns to a company's owners. [9]

treasury bills. A specific type of cash equivalent issued and guaranteed by the U.S. government. [2]

treasury operations. *See* **cash accounting.**

treasury stock. Stock that an insurer in the United States had previously issued, then later repurchased at market price, with the intention of reselling the stock at a later date. [6]

trend. A change that occurs over time. [9]

trend analysis. A type of horizontal analysis that involves calculating percentage changes in financial statement amounts over several successive accounting periods. [9]

trend percentages. *See* **trend analysis.**

turnover ratios. *See* **activity ratios.**

unassigned surplus. For insurers in the United States, the total amount of undistributed and unapportioned surplus remaining in an insurance company since the company began operations. [6]

unassigned surplus funds. *See* **unassigned surplus.**

uncollected income. Income that is due before December 31, but which the insurer has not received as of December 31. [7]

uncollected premiums. Individual life insurance premiums and annuity considerations that are due before the financial reporting date, but the insurer has not received these premiums as of that date. Called premiums outstanding on the Canadian Annual Return. [3]

unearned income. The subset of collected income that has been received but not yet earned. [7]

unearned premium. A portion of the insurance premium received in one period, but applicable to the insurance coverage to be provided in the following period, but before the next policy anniversary date. [7]

unrealized gain (loss). The difference between an asset's book value and its current market value under GAAP or its admitted value under statutory accounting practices. [2]

unrecorded deposits. Deposits that the insurer added to its book balance after the closing date on the bank statement. [3]

valuation. The process of calculating the monetary value of an insurer's assets, liabilities, and owners' equity. [2]

vertical analysis. A type of financial ratio analysis that reveals the relationship of each financial statement item to a specified financial statement item during the same reporting period. [9]

waiver-of-premium benefit. A rider to a life insurance policy that provides premium payments to keep the life insurance policy in force should the insured become disabled and incapable of earning income to pay the premium. [5]

weighted value. An amount that has been multiplied by a percentage in order to account for different risk levels in comparing insurers of different sizes or with different exposures to risk. [9]

Index

An *f* following a page number indicates a Figure or Insight.

A

A. M. Best Company, 155, 162
account form, 5
accounting entry, 22
accounting procedures, changes in, 94
accounting records, 52–53
account payable, 25f, 127
account receivable, 25f, 127
accrual-basis accounting, 109
accrual-basis premium income, 118f
accrued income, 29, 45, 111f, 112f
accumulated cost of insurance, 57f
accumulated value of net premiums, 57f
acquisition expenses, 123f, 125–26
acquisitions, 103
active life reserves, 54
activity ratios, 147f, 148–49, 157f
actuarial assumptions, 51–52
actuary, 51–52
additional paid-in capital, 94, 105
admitted assets, 21, 98, 99, 100f
advance premiums, 84, 133
age of insured, misrepresentation of, 81–82
agent commissions, 85, 126–27
agent salaries, 127–30
agents' commissions due or accrued, 85
aggregate reserves, 52
amortization, 23f, 38, 65–66
amortized cost, 22, 23f
analytical phase (IRIS), 162
annual report, 15
Annual Return, 16
    accrual-basis investment income, 120
    accrued investment income, 45
    capital and surplus on, 106
    CMO accounting, 31
    dividend liabilities reporting, 71
    policy loan accounting, 43
    real estate reporting, 37
    recording premiums waived for disability, 82
    Segregated Funds, 47
    stock categorization, 33f
    used for solvency monitoring, 167
Annual Statement, 15–16
    admitted assets on, 45–46
    asset classification, 21
    CMO accounting, 31
    common stock valuation, 32
    death claims reporting, 80, 82
    deferred premiums unique to, 46

dividend liabilities reporting, 71, 72, 73
    net investment income reported on, 120
    policy loan reporting, 43
    primary basis for solvency monitoring, 161
    real estate reporting, 37
    Separate Accounts, 47
apportioned dividends, 73
appropriated surplus, 96, 106
asset risk, 165f, 168
assets, 4f, 5
    accounting entries, 22–24, 25f
    admitted, 21, 98, 99, 100f
    characteristics, 19–21
    classifications, 20f
    debit balance, 23, 24f
    gains from sale of, 99
    invested, 24–34
    nonadmitted, 21, 99, 100f, 127
    tangible and intangible, 20–21
    term to maturity, 19–20
    valuation, 22, 23f
assigned surplus, 96
association examination, 165
assuming company, 66
assumption reinsurance, 101–2

B

balance sheet, 3–5, 6f, 14
    asset presentation, 19
    displaying net change in cash, 9
    effect of issuing common stock, 92
    effect of issuing preferred stock, 93
    effect of issuing and selling surplus notes, 103
    for mutual insurance company, 52
    results of assumption reinsurance transaction, 102
    vertical analysis, 143–44
balance sheet equation, 4
bank accounts, 43–44
bank errors, 44f
bank reconciliation, 43–44
base period, 142–43
basic accounting equation, 4, 52, 90
bondholder, 27f
bond issuer, 27f
bond principal, 27f
bonds, 20f, 26–30
    discounts and premiums, 30
    insurer-issued, 84
    interest, 29–30
    maturity period, 28
    mortgage-backed, 30–31